Covenant and Community

Covenant and Community

Six Essays on Contemporary Jewish Life and Education

Michael Rosenak

The Jewish Theological Seminary of America   The Melton Centre for Jewish Education

New York and Jerusalem   The Hebrew University of Jerusalem

2013 – 5773

Literary Editor: Vivienne Burstein

ISBN-13: 978-0-87334-008-3

©

Copyright 2013, by
The Jewish Theological Seminary of America
Printing and Binding by S. Nathan Inc.

Jewish Education Series, volume 6

The Jewish Education Series:

To my family

Contents

Jonathan Cohen: Introducing the Essays

Michael Rosenak, a founder of the academic discipline known as the Philosophy of Jewish Education, has once again presented us with a most challenging and important book. The essays contained in this volume should command the attention of a number of audiences: students of modern Jewish thought, contemporary Jewish thinkers and, perhaps most importantly – Jewish educational leaders. In his earlier works, *Commandments and Concerns* and *Roads to the Palace*, Prof. Rosenak set a new standard for discourse and deliberation on Jewish educational issues in the modern setting. In *Tree of Life, Tree of Knowledge*, he played a key role in the derivation of philosophical-educational insights from canonical texts. In his long and productive career at the Hebrew University's Melton Centre for Jewish Education and the Mandel Leadership Institute, Mike – as he is called by both colleagues and students – has dedicated himself to articulating the relation between two complex and problematic areas: theology and education.

Both theology and education, in and of themselves, have been beset by an extended identity crisis. Theology has had to define its uniqueness vis-à-vis the very resources that it must draw upon for its sustenance: religious faith and philosophy. As for education, it is a practical pursuit that must give rise to decisions as to what should and can be successfully imparted to the young. Yet in order to conduct its business responsibly, it must have recourse to knowledge encased in multiple disciplines operating under plural paradigms. As will become clear in the essays that follow, Rosenak presents challenges to theology and education alike. Theology must "ring true" and testify to genuine religious experience. It must likewise be coherent (free as much as possible from contradictions) and plausible to moderns in light of "all else they know to be true". Education must be rooted in a principled world-view as well as in visions of the educated person and an "educated public". It should also present overall strategies and concrete suggestions for moving from perceived reality to desirable ends. As far as the interaction between the two fields is concerned – theological insights must be "translated" into educational terms. For example, certain theological ideals – seemingly worthy in themselves – can, under certain communal and educational conditions, lead to the development of stunted personalities or prove decidedly counterproductive to the cultivation of the "ideally" educated person.

The essays in this volume testify to Rosenak's talent for written expression in both the narrative and conceptual modes. In keeping with his demand that theology be rooted in testimony – the book is replete with poignant and illuminating stories that manage to capture important aspects of the human experience and contemporary Jewish condition. In keeping with his other demand, however, that theology not remain content with testimony, the reader will find Rosenak reflecting on the stories he has told by way of penetrating and sometimes difficult conceptual distinctions. The reader is urged to take the time to digest these distinctions and contemplate them before "moving on". Second and third readings of crucial passages inevitably bring their rewards in enhanced understanding and further appreciation of Rosenak's subtle and complex insights.

The aim of the first essay of the book is to justify the theological orientation of the work as a whole. According to Rosenak, the well-known alternatives of "ethnicity" or "spirituality" are not adequate in making sense of contemporary Jewish experience. There is a need for the kind of committed reflection that only theology can provide. Characteristically, however, this first essay, which is a reflection on the very place of theology in Judaism, begins with a charming yet sophisticated story about two recognizable "types" of Jews. One, originally from Pinsk, is still in love with the rhythms, cadences and colors of Jewish life – even though he has long since lost his belief in God, revelation and other tenets of classical Jewish faith. He sees no reason why he cannot go on living a rich Jewish life without the ballast of faith or theology. The other, originally from Minsk, is also an "apikorus", but a much more principled one. He has actually stopped living the tradition. Still, he is not satisfied with this negative gesture. He feels he must believe in his unbelief – that he should be capable of articulating it and justifying it. He seeks out the "Pinsker" in order to obtain guidance in understanding the meaning of his "apikorsut". Naturally – the "Minsker" is sorely disappointed by the Pinsker's unwillingness to provide the "negative theology" of unbelief he so urgently desires. Rosenak, however, does not leave us with this narrative vignette. He then proceeds to analyze the attitudes of the Pinsker and the Minsker by way of conceptual categories taken from the thought of Ernst Simon (a student of Buber and Rosenzweig and the first Director of the Hebrew University's School of Education). It is here that he introduces the unlikely concepts of "Catholic" and "Protestant" Judaism – the first being the kind of Judaism that encompasses one's whole life-sphere (perhaps unreflectively) and the second the kind which has come to be regarded as only one facet of human "culture" (and which therefore must constantly reflect on its relation to the other facets). These two overarching categories are then further applied to an analysis of four types of modern Jews – Ultra-Orthodox, Cultural Zionists, Political Zionists and Modern Orthodox. In both his narrative and conceptual discourse, it is clear that Rosenak has been influenced by the typological thinking of R. Joseph B. Soloveitchik, and that he has a clear affinity to the Modern Orthodox type. Further, while he may have sympathized in his youth with the attitude of the Pinsker, he clearly states that this brand of "heimische" Judaism cannot meaningfully survive and flourish without the reflective explication and justification sought by the Minsker. "More Jews doing Jewish" is simply not enough.

While the first essay seeks to legitimize and valorize theological reflection as a crucial component of Jewish culture transmission, the second essay begins with a cultural-educational problem and then demonstrates the importance of theological reflection for the clarification and constructive tackling of that problem. The problem is the issue of "translation", namely: can Jewish canonical texts, replete as they are with religious assumptions and perspectives, be "translated" such that they can speak the language of modern secularity without doing violence to the "original"? Certain Jewish educational thinkers, such as Isaiah Liebowitz, have claimed that any translation of Jewish texts to the discourse of contemporary humanism must necessarily distort their content. The texts should be allowed to speak for themselves and their theocentric perspectives should remain intact. Other thinkers, such as David Hartman, have emphasized the virtues of translation as a medium for creating commonality between religious and secular Jews. Michael Rosenak – while not negating translation as both a valuable and necessary educational gesture – is careful to remind us of its limits, and warns us against the kind of reductionism that relates to biblical transcendence as a human "construction". We must engage in "partial translation", fully aware of what is lost as well as what is gained in the process.

Like the previous essay, this essay also begins with two stories taken from the author's own rich educational experience. In both stories, we hear of educators who try to "translate" biblical passages to pupils such that they might speak to the children's supposedly modern sensibilities. Little do the teachers know that the pupils are "wise" to their attempt to explain (for example) a biblical figure's sense of having lost the "spirit of God" by a simple reference to his psychological condition at the time ("he was in a state of clinical depression"). Students, whether religious or secular, could expect to be "led into another world" when confronting the Bible, and might not wish to have biblical transcendence reduced to human psychological states.

13

Again, in this essay as well, Rosenak's narrative prelude is followed by a more conceptual and systematic exposition. We are first exposed to the ambivalent position of Shlomo Goitein, the renowned biblical scholar and educator. While Goitein retained (from his Orthodox upbringing) an Orthopraxis lifestyle and a high level of respect for the theocentric piety of the Bible and of subsequent tradition – he could not in good conscience appropriate the traditional theology for himself. On occasion he would inveigh against "translating" the Bible into humanistic categories as a distortion of its "original spirit" (a "spirit" he had imbibed and still valued). At other times, he would maintain, in a manner similar to Ahad Ha'am, that God should be understood as the "spirit of Israel", or as Israel's perception of the Rock upon which this spirit rests. At this point, Rosenak enters the discussion actively and expresses his opposition to positing God as a "projection" of the human spirit. The moral and educational upshot of such a reduction is, he maintains, nothing less than the absolutization of the human spirit when, in truth, from a biblical perspective, there must be a transcendent Source that **judges** and **limits** the human spirit.

In his discussion of the views of Goitein, Rosenak introduces the valuable distinction between translation on the basis of "truth-claims" and translation for "pedagogical" reasons. In the first case, the "translator" cannot identify with the (transcendent) truth-claims of the original and therefore must "translate" them into terms that are more consonant with his/her own (modern, humanistic) principles. In the second case, the "translation" is made out of consideration for the messages that the **pupils** can or cannot sustain – given their stage of psychological development, their social circumstances or their assumed beliefs. I believe this distinction can aid both educational policy-makers and classroom teachers in understanding their own educational decisions and actions.

Rosenak concludes this essay by referring the reader to the cultural-educational perspective of another complex Jew: Franz Rosenzweig. Rosenzweig, like Max Otto and Buber, calls upon moderns to hold themselves open to the possibility of an experience of the Holy – a dimension not reducible to the human perspective and actually intent upon **changing** that perspective. Certainly, for self-aware, sophisticated moderns who do not live under the aspect of "false consciousness", the experience of transcendence cannot be unreflective and all-encompassing – lest they abandon something of their authenticity as moderns. Nonetheless – the "voice" of the transcendent can be heard in and through the teachings and practices of Jewish culture. For both religious **and** humanistic reasons, national culture cannot present itself to education as a self-sufficient, uncritical norm. Culture must point beyond itself so that it itself may be judged. The transmission of culture is a necessary condition for Jewish education – for it is through the texts and practices of the tradition that the commanding voice of judgment may speak. But it is not a sufficient condition, lest transcendence be forgotten and humans be educated to worship only the work of their hands. It is clear that Rosenak identifies strongly with this Rosenzweigian injunction. By the end of the essay, Rosenak even expresses the wish that educators "translate" Jewish culture as little as possible, thereby allowing the traditional forms the "freedom" to "point beyond themselves".

The third and fourth essays of this volume move from typologies of Jewish experience and belief confronting the modern Jewish individual to "epoch-making events" that have had an indelibly profound effect on the Jewish people as a whole: the Holocaust and the persistent survival and flourishing of the State of Israel against overwhelming odds. The essays are deliberately not arranged in chronological order. In the third essay, Rosenak concerns himself with theological reactions to the Six Day War, while in the fourth he discusses theological responses to the Holocaust and their educational implications. The reason for this is that Rosenak wishes first to examine possible contemporary reactions to what has been perceived by some to be an overt revelation of God's presence, and only afterwards to consider a range of responses to the experience of His absence.

True to the pattern displayed until now, the author begins the third essay with narrative "testimonies" – only later moving on to systematic "theology". So-called "religious" and so-called "secular" Jews tell of their experiences in the wake of the Six Day War and Israel's astounding victory. As we read these arresting testimonies, it becomes clear that conventional distinctions between "religious" and "secular" perspectives are being called into question – as the issue of what "counts" as a genuine, legitimate or authentic "religious" response to the event is radically re-opened. Pointed questions are presented to all of these "witnesses", and no one insight or pronouncement is regarded as providing all the answers. Finally – one main question is extrapolated from this "testimonial" part of the essay, namely: how can we make sense of the relation between the "sacred" past and future of Judaism and the exigencies of the historical present? It is on the basis of this tension-ridden question that the "theological" part of the treatise unfolds.

Six possible theological responses are then articulated and evaluated, on the assumption that all testimony must be complemented by reflection. Modern Jews are called upon to deliberate rationally in order to determine the most reasonable way to interpret "epoch-making" historical events. The first response is termed "active messianism" and is identified with the position of Gush Emunim. According to this view, the Six Day War "teaches" that all of the sacred Land of Israel has been redeemed by way of an overt divine miracle. This makes it a heinous crime to even consider setting the clock of redemption backward by offering to return "sacred" territory in exchange for the illusion of peace. According to one extreme version of this perspective – God has tested the Jewish people three times, during the War of Independence, the Sinai Campaign and again in the wake of the Six Day War. Each time the Jewish people was prevailed upon by the "world" to relinquish territory in exchange for "peace". The first two times – Jewish acquiescence to the demands of the "world" actually resulted in another war, rather than peace. Should the Jewish people give in to these demands a third time –

another, even more destructive war will ensue. He who seeks peace must retain the territories, rather than give them up.

The second theological response presented by Rosenak, and attributed to the distinguished religious Israeli diplomat Yaacov Herzog, also stands in genuine awe at the miraculousness of the establishment of the State and of its uncanny victory in the Six Day War. Unlike in the position of Gush Emunim, however, this wondrous turning of God's face to the Jewish people is perceived as challenging us to conduct ourselves with moral sensitivity and responsibility – in the **hope** that this might really be the beginning of the redemption.

Yet a third response is attributed to certain rabbinical figures and religious groups not really identified with Religious Zionism. While certainly acknowledging the miraculous nature of the victory, they do not see it as sign of the sanctity or unique religious quality of the present historical or political situation. They rather interpret it as further evidence of God's providence and Israel's dependence. The wondrous aspect of the event is that it allows Jews to continue to remember their sacred past and pray for their sacred future.

A fourth response is termed "Zionist Moral Halakhism". Like the first view, it regards the events ensuing from the Six Day War as constituting a test for the Jewish people. The test, however, is not whether or not Jews will cling to their sacred land – but whether or not they will conduct themselves according to the moral principles embedded in the Halakha – particularly towards those "others" in the territories for whose welfare we are now responsible. This group asks: now that we have been given the capacity to offer territory for peace – will we answer this call or pursue self-centered messianic aggrandizement?

Rosenak's fifth response, identified most particularly with the iconoclastic thinker Isaiah Liebowitz, is called "Zionist Negation of Religious-Political Significance". On the one hand, Leibowitz approves of the Zionist project from a "secular" perspective – as freeing the Jews from the yoke of their latter-day oppressors and allowing them political autonomy. On the other hand, he staunchly refuses to attribute any miraculous or messianic significance to the reality of the State of Israel, its victories – and least of all, its conquests.

Finally, we are presented with a sixth approach – called "Anti-Zionist Negation of Religious-Political Significance". This is the approach of the Neturei Karta and its ilk, wherein the very existence of the State and its seeming victories are regarded as the work of the devil. The test this time is whether Jews will be led astray by statehood, military victory and other forms of "goyim naches", or continue, as our forefathers did, to patiently await the truly miraculous and supernatural coming of the Messiah.

It is clear that Rosenak identifies most with the second and the fourth position, although he presents all perspectives with some degree of sympathy and fairness. It is important to read and re-read Rosenak's description of each view in detail in order to obtain a real sense of the ethos and logic underlying each position. The author's hope is that readers will be moved by the testimony and intellectually stimulated by the different models of theological reflection – and thereby encouraged to find their own theological responses to recent events on the basis of a thorough awareness of the alternatives.

The third essay, then, presents us with a series of possible ways to make theological sense of great events in which God's providence seems, at least to some, to be almost tangibly **present**. While this is no simple matter – since "event" theologies promulgated in the wake of military success can readily lead to self-congratulation and triumphalism, it would seem virtually impossible, if not downright obscene – to take upon oneself the task of making theological "sense" of the Holocaust; that "event" wherein God was perhaps most "tangibly" felt to be **absent**. Thus Rosenak begins the fourth essay by re-opening the question of the necessity and legitimacy of theology; he quotes Irving Greenberg's stricture that "theological discussion is not permissible in the presence of burning children". Perhaps, after the Holocaust, Jews should confine themselves to responsible historical study of the causes of the catastrophe and the cultivation of a sense of ethnic solidarity. Nonetheless, Rosenak insists, an anti-theological response is itself a kind of reverse "theology", with its own absolutes and dogmas – and theological grappling with the Holocaust should not be regarded a priori as less legitimate than its alternative.

As in the previous essay, Rosenak sets forth a range of possible theological responses to an "epoch-making event".

In the third essay, Rosenak does not address himself directly to the educational implications of the various positions discussed (although the views themselves are sufficiently suggestive as to allow the sensitive reader to undertake this on his/her own). In the fourth essay, however, he overtly seeks to "translate" theology to education, such that the educational "gains" or "losses" of any particular approach become more readily apparent. For example, he asks: which of the articulated approaches can beget, in their adherents, a sense of trust even in the broken life that we live, with all its flaws and injustices – generating an ability to see "hidden miracles" even in a terribly flawed world? Which of the approaches can serve to cultivate "hope" – namely: that attitude that looks to the day when reality **as it is** will actually be "overcome"? What is the price of engendering "trust" without "hope", or "hope" without "trust"? Are there genuinely theological approaches that do not contain the resources for the development of either "hope" **or** trust? Can any Jewish education worthy of the name allow for the growth of young people who are bereft of either of these attitudes? What kind of personality can or cannot grow under the aegis of this or that orientation? Can "open" persons grow in surroundings where it is assumed that the world is a basically hostile place? These are distinctly educational questions, and Rosenak addresses them through the prism of what the well-known philosopher of education, Joseph Schwab, has called the "commonplaces" of the educational situation – the learner, the teacher, the milieu (or context surrounding the educational situation) and the subject matter. For example, he asks: does a given approach lead to parity between the commonplaces, or does it give any one of them undue priority?

The five positions presented as candidates for educational translation in the fourth essay are as follows:

1 – The claim that even in the aftermath of the Holocaust, nothing is really wrong with the relationship between God and Israel. Certain ultra-Orthodox or ultra-Zionist ideologues have maintained that it is the masses of the Jewish people who should be taken to task, and not God. Instead of remaining steadfast in their traditional faith, Jews succumbed to the seductive call of Emancipation. Instead of leaving Europe en masse in order to build a new life in Eretz Israel, Jews insisted on remaining in Europe and blinded themselves to the oncoming disaster.

2 – There is something definitely wrong with the relationship between God and Israel in the wake of the Holocaust. One can no longer speak of God's "saving presence" as pertinent in any way to the horrors of Auschwitz. It would be blasphemous to attribute any divine plan or purpose to the cataclysm. Nonetheless, writes Emil Fackenheim – one of the main exponents of this approach according to Rosenak, it is possible to hear a "commanding presence" speaking out of the ashes and sounding a "614th commandment", namely: we are enjoined not to give Hitler posthumous victories by allowing the Jewish people to wither away. All Jews, of whatever stripe or belief, must now dedicate themselves to the survival and flourishing of the Jewish people.

3 – While something definitely seems wrong in the relationship between God and Israel – there is nothing **ultimately** wrong. What we have here is a classic case of God's hiding His face – according to Norman Lamm, or a case of God restraining His hand in order to allow human beings unrestrained free will – according to Eliezer Berkovits. For Soloveitchik, the Holocaust is indeed inexplicable, and this differentiates his approach from that of the ultra-Orthodox and the ultra-Zionists. But, says Soloveitchik, in Jewish tradition, catastrophes are to be met with collective self-examination and self-improvement, and not futile attempts at understanding. For Isaiah Leibowitz, history is meaningless anyway and there is no such thing as hope. The only gesture that has value is the disinterested worship of God under any and all conditions. One might question whether all these thinkers, who are so different as regards their most fundamental principles, should be included in one "camp". Yet Rosenak's grouping of them under one rubric with respect to their Holocaust theology is certainly thought-provoking and original.

4 – There is something definitely and really wrong in the covenantal relationship between God and Israel. This view, attributed to Eliezer Schweid, claims that the Holocaust places too great a strain on the Covenant for it to be retained in anything like traditional form. The Covenant creates expectations of both sides, and when one side is so blatantly absent when His presence is most needed, the ensuing catastrophe cannot be merely assimilated to the pluses and minuses of the historical

"balance sheet". The relationship with the transcendent must somehow be constituted on new terms. We can no longer expect that God will intervene in history on our behalf. Perhaps we can still hope that he will support and sustain our own human efforts to mend this broken world.

5 – The fifth and last position discussed by Rosenak in this context is the "anti-theological theology" of the radical Rabbi Richard Rubenstein. For Rubenstein, the entire structure of the traditional Jewish belief system must be called into question. God has not merely been silent. In the aftermath of the horrors of the Holocaust, he must be regarded as dead. This, however, does not mean the end of Judaism. The role of ultimate leadership must now pass to human beings. Further, the human will to realize the commandments in an indifferent world takes on an even greater significance.

As mentioned above, the third and fourth essays in the book confront the reader with diverse theological reactions to major historical events; events that have affected the Jews **as a people** in a most fundamental way. The fifth essay proceeds to analyze the very experience and concept of "Peoplehood" itself. As Rosenak mentions, the cultivation of a sense of peoplehood, with its concurrent responsibilities, has gained a great deal of currency as a Jewish educational desideratum in recent times. From what Rosenak calls a "descriptive" point of view, many Jews do indeed regard themselves as part of a people that is often singled out and persecuted. They might also be proud of the dignity with which their ancestors and contemporaries have borne, and continue to bear, the many indignities that seem all too often to go with merely being Jewish. Still – while such an ethos does create a sense of commonality, and has the advantage of not demanding adherence to defined beliefs and practices, it lacks a sense of positive, existential purpose. On the other hand, when Jewish peoplehood is looked at "prescriptively", as tied to a certain destiny or task in the world, disagreement immediately sets in as to what that destiny and task (if there be such) actually is. This is the problematic with which the fifth essay begins.

Further on in the essay, Rosenak critiques the cultural-educational orientation that would content itself with the transmission of a sense of belonging to a historically persecuted group. Such an approach, maintains Rosenak, can only flourish under conditions of tension between Jews and their surroundings. Using Soloveitchik's terms, he insists that the orientation of the "Covenant of Fate" is not enough to sustain meaningful Jewish identity. A "Covenant of Destiny", wherein the Jew understands him/herself as bidden to realize a definite purpose in the world, is also needed to generate and maintain the motivation to be different in an open society. Drawing on a distinction taken from the writings of the philosopher Nathan Rotenstreich, Rosenak critiques the curriculum of "passive history", wherein the student is shown how Jews have **reacted** to what was done to them by others in the past. He prefers the curriculum of "active history", wherein social and intellectual movements are depicted as originating in a native Jewish inventiveness and creativity.

Michael Rosenak

Continuing his critique, Rosenak maintains that those who would educate for "descriptive" peoplehood assume that this is the only way to reinvigorate Jewish allegiance in an era when modernity and enlightenment threaten to overrun religion. The Jews, so it is claimed, are assimilating and dying out. Increased modernization and secularization are irreversibly eroding the beliefs and practices of the Jewish tradition. Under these conditions, when the rehabilitation of tradition seems impossible, only a heightened sense of "peoplehood" can perhaps go some way towards slowing the process. Rosenak, the incorrigible optimist, feels that this diagnosis should not go unchallenged. There are, he writes, many signs of positive, Jewish cultural revitalization that seem to refute the gloomy predictions of Marshall Sklare and his ilk. The rebirth of the Hebrew language, the flowering of Hebrew literature, the advent and proliferation of Torah study among women – along with many other phenomena – would seem to point to the possibility of a positive Jewish cultural revival. Not only that: it is precisely the interaction with modernity that has provided the leaven for the growth of these developments. At this point, Rosenak has recourse once again to his skills as a narrator as he vividly describes the organization of a public *minyan* in the Warsaw airport (a phenomenon that would have been unthinkable before the advent of the State of Israel) as well as the case of a young Russian student from Odessa who makes the long trip to Moscow to interview for a premier Jewish education fellowship in Jerusalem.

In presenting his own, positive point of view on this issue, Rosenak wishes neither to remain content with "descriptive peoplehood" nor to suggest any one specific "destiny" that all Jews should appropriate for themselves. He rather wishes to engage Jews in the contemporary argument and dialogue surrounding the question of positive Jewish norms. In keeping with the spirit of Franz Rosenzweig, who once again proves to be his mentor in this context, Rosenak hopes that contemporary Jews might be educated such that they choose to commit themselves to the sympathetic exploration of the Jewish past. The educated Jew, for Rosenak, is one for whom "nothing Jewish is alien". This should be done, however, without closing any options as to what the Jewish present and future might look like. Jews of different stripes will of necessity access different resources from the tradition as the basis for their own beliefs and practices. They should be encouraged to appropriate as much of the tradition as they "can", but without violation of their personal authenticity and with no a priori restrictions as to the outcome. Such an education can only take place in a spirit that blends both commitment and pluralism. Yet, writes Rosenak, it might very well be that as students discover the incredible plurality that has characterized the Jewish tradition in the past, the phenomenon of contemporary Jewish pluralism will come to seem less discontinuous and more genuine.

We have come to a point, then, wherein it has been established that **mere** peoplehood, without a positive content that **justifies** it, cannot serve as the ultimate goal of Jewish education. The final essay of this book, then, is dedicated to the question of the **content** of Jewish life. Abraham Joshua Heschel has famously claimed that Jews have never been recognized, neither by themselves nor by others, as a people specializing in the artistic design of **space**. Jews are better known for their ability to construct "castles in **time**". In keeping with this characterization, Rosenak, in discussing the kind of content that has shaped the life of the Jewish people, takes us on a journey through the Jewish calendar.

Within the framework of this journey through the Jewish year, Rosenak chooses to focus on two months – the month of Nissan with its Passover festival, and the month of Tishrei – bearer of the New Year festival, the fast of Yom Kippur and the Sukkot holiday, punctuated by special celebrations on the eighth day – Shemini Atzeret and Simchat Torah. In keeping with an educational orientation first developed within the framework of the Melton Centre's Jewish Values Project, a curriculum project headed by Rosenak in the late '70s and early '80s (originally designed for Jewish schools in the Diaspora), Rosenak prefers not to portray the festivals of the Jewish calendar as mere occasions for the observance of "customs and ceremonies". He rather seeks to uncover the values and virtues that underlie the texts and practices associated with the holiday. Nissan, for Rosenak, becomes the month that emphasizes **particularism**, that orientation whereby a people expresses its "need to be itself, to define itself, to find its own freedom". This is distinguished from **radical particularism**, a posture that regards any concern with the larger human family as "naïve" or "self-hating". It is the month when the interests and fate of the Jew and the "other" (in this case the Egyptian) run counter to each other. The Egyptians are smitten with plagues and drowned in the

Red Sea, and the Israelites are saved. Tishrei, on the other hand, becomes the month that emphasizes **universalism,** an attitude that prioritizes solidarity with all of mankind as the ultimate aim of any particular, national striving. This is distinguished from **radical universalism,** or the de-legitimization of any concern with the well-being of ethnic or national groups as "parochial" and "self-serving". On Rosh Hashanah, all humans are judged equally as they pass under the crook of the divine shepherd. In the famous Haftara of Jonah, read at the afternoon service of Yom Kippur, God has mercy on the sinners of Nineveh and retracts his punishment when they genuinely repent (in contrast to the watery doom inflicted on the Egyptians). On Sukkot, sacrifices are brought for the 70 nations of the world. On the Shabbat of Chol HaMoed Sukkot, the book of Ecclesiastes is read, a book with a definite universal-existential cast.

In order that the values underlying the structure of the calendar be presented in all their living complexity, however, Rosenak insists on emphasizing two other aspects of the rhythm of Jewish time. First, within the framework of major holidays themselves, there are built-in correctives that prevent us from being carried away by either particularism or universalism. On Passover, we spill drops of wine to express our regret at the death of Egyptians in the Red Sea, signifying that our national redemption cannot be really complete if it comes at the price of human life. On the Shavuot holiday, considered by the sages to be the "Atzeret", or "stopping point" of the Passover holiday, we are called upon to remember the midrashic story wherein

God offers the Torah to all the nations before offering it to Israel – as well as the passage that describes the Torah as having been written in the seventy languages of the nations. In Tishrei, on the other hand, a particularistic corrective is needed against the possible excesses of universalism. After the seventy sacrifices that have been offered for the welfare of the nations on Sukkot, the Jewish people offers its own particular sacrifice and takes part in an intimate, "family" celebration on Shemini Atzeret. The prayer for rain offered on that day is attuned to the weather cycle of the Land of Israel alone.

For Rosenak – this dialectical back-and-forth motion, balancing a healthy particularism with a healthy universalism, is not only concentrated within the rhythm of the major festivals alone. It can be found scattered all over the calendar – as, for example, on Chanukah – where the celebration of the victory of the Maccabees is balanced by the words of the prophet Zecharia who proclaims that God achieves His purposes not by way of His might, but by way of His spirit. Most importantly for Rosenak, values associated with holidays must not be enacted only on those holidays – but must become features of the rhythm of Jewish life all year round. Jews are called upon to live the dialectic of particularism and universalism in all their doings: to be both loyal to their tribe and willing to judge it from a universal perspective, to be actively concerned with global welfare but to realize that "the poor of one's own city have priority".

The content of the life of the Jewish people, then, consists of season-bound observances that represent values and attitudes that are meant to inform life as a whole. It is only as such that they are prevented from becoming mere shows and posturings that have no real relation to the rest of what one does. In this connection, Rosenak, for a final time, shows his strength as a raconteur when he retells, at the very beginning of the essay, a story by Stephen Leacock describing a Mother's Day celebration empty of any real content, since the family members have never shown any real regard for Mother at any time.

In charting the trajectory of this volume, we have only been able to give a foretaste and a brief outline of its rich and stimulating content. We once again advise the reader to proceed slowly and deliberately through both the narrative and conceptual sections of the essays, so as not to lose subtle nuances that are often crucial to a full understanding of what the author is trying to say. The book is best read by readers that already have a penchant for plurality and complexity. It is not meant for those who prefer open-and-shut answers to black and white questions. Theology by itself is a complex subject, as is education. The interaction between these two realms generates even more complexity. Under Michael Rosenak's guidance, however, this unique meeting between two disciplines of commitment can provide much illumination and wisdom of the kind so sorely needed in Jewish educational discourse today. In these essays, Rosenak is again contributing his most penetrating insights to scholars and practitioners alike.

Preface

This book is concerned with testimonies to the Jewish experience of God in the modern era. The question that preoccupies us is whether the perhaps scandalous claim to a special bond between the universal God and the people of Israel, can still be maintained in the light of modern consciousness. What counts as evidence for religious commitment and hope and what speaks against it? Who shall decide what testifies to the veracity of the religious view of the world and what counts against it? Moreover, in terms of today's human spirit, what difference does it make? It is a task of theology to suggest ways of answering these questions, or at least of relating to them with integrity.

These are interlocking essays. They all have to do with transcendence, identity and contemporary Jewish consciousness. In a sense they deal with disparate issues, but they are all about modern Jews. But that is not all they have in common. All of them are indebted to John Dewey's conception of the philosophy of education insofar as they all believe that philosophy is an enterprise of the integration of various experiences that are searching for wholeness of some kind. Perhaps conversely, all of them have theological foundations, by which I mean that questions of God and Israel are viewed as indispensible to an understanding of Jewish existence. All are concerned on an educational level with the issue of translation, i.e. they all strive for comprehensibility in order that young people be brought into the circle of history and culture. All of them attempt to avoid sermonizing, and none of them is the enemy of enquiry.

My book is not meant to be a learned treatise but related essays in theology and/or education, both of which are concerned with theoretical subjects to be mastered and with personal concerns to be addressed. I shall spell out one such concern that I hope will point to the task I have undertaken and its tenor.

As a young adolescent in New York City, I was an enthusiastic member of a Zionist youth movement called Hashomer Hadati which, already in Europe, had split off from the radically socialist Hashomer Hatza'ir movement. Even then, it had become clear to the religiously-observant members of Hashomer Hatza'ir that their parent movement had radically distanced itself from traditional belief and practice and that it could not be a congenial home to Orthodox youths. Yet, they kept the faith on socialism and, like the secularists of Hashomer Hatza'ir, believed themselves to be rebelling against the bourgeois conventions of their parents. They did this not by throwing off the yoke of religious life and its traditional norms, but by carrying them to their 'consistent' conclusions. (In the process they discovered that no rebellion against parents is more delectable than standing up to them in the name of their own ideals!) We believed that the more stringent our practice, the more righteous we were. Others, no doubt, saw us as *self*-righteous and exasperating.

One of the stringencies of Sabbath observance that many of the *haverim* ("comrades") took upon themselves was the prohibition against carrying objects, any objects, in what

Jewish law defines as "the public domain". Hence, so as not to carry handkerchiefs ("objects") in the street (the "public domain"), we took to wearing them around our necks, thereby transforming them into scarves which, as clothing worn rather than objects carried, did no apparent injury to the Talmudic law.

When I first appeared at our Sabbath table with a handkerchief-scarf around my neck, my father turned to me with an expression of guarded sarcasm. "And what is this all about?" I was prepared. "Dad, we make no compromises about Sabbath observance in the movement." "And tell me," he asked, as though simply curious or perhaps examining, in a gingerly fashion, an anthropological curiosity, "What happens after the first time you blow your nose?!" I have forgotten my answer but I imagine that it was vague – and sanctimonious. I was angry.

On the following morning, we left the house together on our separate ways to different synagogues (mine was a youth service consisting mainly of Hashomer Hadati youngsters, unlike the 'bourgeois' place my father attended). Before we separated, my father turned to me and summed up what he had to say on the subject of our conversation of the previous evening: "Michael, never make Judaism appear to be ridiculous. Don't cause people to laugh at it."

I realized, even then, that there were different ways of understanding my father's remark. Judged least charitably, he might have been afraid of what Gentiles would think, and feared their ridicule. Or, as a person of great aesthetic sensibility, he might have meant that what is ugly to him was surely distasteful to God as well. Or perhaps he thought that the sages were right when they said that there is no greater transgression than to profane God's name by uncouth behavior that prevents Jews as well as Gentiles from acknowledging His holiness, from perceiving Him as the source of beauty, of civil association and of moral values.

At the time, of course, I thought he meant the first: he was afraid of what people might say. That was of course unacceptable to me. Who was he to decide what was ridiculous? That was the way of assimilation! Was he a rabbinic authority? A scholar or religious thinker who could survey, define and delineate the halakhic issues at stake?

When I think of it now, I believe he was guided by the desire to avoid the transgression of *Hilul HaShem*, the desecration of God's name, which he saw as interwoven with his code of ethics, his sense of order and rationality, with his aesthetic sensibility and with his historical loyalty.

While I am still not certain which he meant, I believe the time has come to think again about my father's request – as a Jewish teacher, as my parents' son. These essays have continued, at least from my current perspective, the conversation initiated one wintry night in 1946.

Introduction:
Who Needs Theology?[*]

This is a book about issues and questions that arise in Jewish education – in its broadest philosophical sense – whenever there is a perceived dissonance between what Jews experience, and what they are told they should believe in the realm of faith and doctrine. It makes no attempt to provide definitive answers to such questions and I present no systematic statement of 'what Judaism teaches'. I am not qualified to do this. My concern is with the role of theology, as we shall shortly delineate it, in modern Jewish life, whether defined as 'religious' or not. I point to some ways to locate these questions and dilemmas, and to explore them through the eyes of varying kinds of Jews, in discrete situations, with diverse subject matters. For better or for worse, this task of location and exploration, I shall argue, owes much to theological thinking.

I shall also argue that theological thinking is set off from both doctrinal statements, to be believed and unquestionably defended, on the one hand, and from philosophical thought that allegedly approaches its subjects without set truths and convictions, on the other. How it is different from each is a central concern of all that follows.

The difficulty with theological-educational discourse is that it dare not negate the uses of philosophy; nor may it give up the defense of religion. For some time I have thought about writing about this tension, but, never sure that I would not fall off the ledges of apologetics and cold analysis, I put it off. Though my professional life has centered on the teaching of philosophies of education, I was accustomed to examining concepts, theories and practices, generally analyzing and comparing them with alleged detachment and precision, as though I were 'above' them.

While the subjects to be discussed are approached through conceptual categories that meet standards of rationality and plausibility, here I have no intention of being the academic. I wish rather to deal with theological issues, that is, questions that point to God in history and in the experience of the contemporary individual – and that concern me as an educator. Hence the problem. On the one hand, the focus is on theological issues that have made a difference in my life and in the life of my community of faith, and that could shape educational enterprises. On the other hand, this is not intended to be a personal confession or preachment.

And so, my project is problematic. It seems too personal and too suffused with conviction and fervor for the treatise of a reasoning theorist. It could be interpreted by 'serious' scholars as an escape from (intellectual) freedom, to paraphrase Erich Fromm. Conversely, among the devout, my 'academic' interest in Judaism and its manifold forms of articulation and transmission threatens always to make me an outsider, with outsider perceptions, classifications and analyses.

There is a deep-seated bias prevalent among believing persons against theology. Theology, it is said, might be useful and suitable for non-Jews who lived by faiths and doctrines that required constant defense and explication. For Jews, among whom actions and not beliefs come first, this is said to be superfluous. Judaism, so it is said, is 'a way of life' which requires little reflection. Hence, it made sense to declare that Jewish education was about socialization. 'Doing' was the text of Jewish life; thinking about it, the often superfluous footnote.

This approach was particularly persuasive to traditional Jews whose adherents include modern and contemporary Jewry. There have been, in the generations since the eighteenth century "Enlightenment", those who sought to maintain continuity and loyalty yet were skeptical about dogmatic verities and enthusiasms. They became what the twentieth century thinker, Abraham Joshua Heschel, called "religious behaviorists",[1] doing the tradition but largely untouched by it and brushing off theological concerns. There were (and are) the markedly loyal persons who were threatened by the convictions and modes of discourse of the liberal public domain. There (unfortunately!) one could hear a multitude of plausible arguments, whether articulated or simply assumed, for a variety of enticing ideas and ideologies. Hence, the idea that Judaism was "a way of life" was a conviction of refuge. What counted was practice, not theory; not talking but doing; not arguing but testifying to faith. It was only many years later that I discovered how damaging a disdain for theory can be for practice.

The above may well seem strange and indefensible. Does not the ultra-Orthodox world pay ample attention to beliefs and to the inculcation of appropriate world views? These world views are not, however, called theology or recognized as such; they go under the name of *hashkafah*, the inculcation of the right way to think. *Hashkafah* might be profound and multifaceted, and it echoes the dissimilar views of diverse rabbis and schools of thought. Yet it is, all in all, less inclined to individuality, less friendly to dialectical discourse and disinclined to make hard questions accessible to people outside the inner circles of learning and leadership.

The Modern Orthodox exposition of *hashkafah* is different from the ultra-Orthodox (Haredi) kind because, on the margins of the conversation, there *is* a kind of theology. This discourse is often dogmatic in tone and substance (*'hashkafic'*) but it comes together with, at least, a cautious respect for theological questions. This Modern Orthodoxy's (generally wary) participation in the world of theology might take off from biblical dilemmas (e.g., the sufferings of the righteous Job), or from rabbinic midrash studied as a source of profound questions, or from medieval exegesis translated into contemporary categories of modern Jewish thought. And yet it is unique insofar as it makes serious use of halakhic literature in clarifying theological issues.

Typical of a Modern Orthodox approach in which *hahkafah* was beginning to encounter theology, was a pithy but heavily nuanced comment attributed to Rabbi Samson Raphael Hirsch, the founder of neo-Orthodoxy in nineteenth century Germany. Heinrich Graetz, Hirsch's one time student who was to become a noted historian, had come to visit the older man and had confided in him that he was undergoing great turmoil in the domain of religious faith. Hirsch's mild and bemused reaction was that a person who wished to travel around and explore the whole world also had to have a look at the North Pole! In other words, while everything is open to purview, this should not influence how people should behave as Orthodox Jews. They would be expected to be loyal.

And mixing metaphor with historical fact: many young Jews did make their ways around the world, often getting off the train in such centers of culture as Berlin, Paris and Oxford (and today Mumbai and Bangkok), with only some returning to the havens of Jewish life such as Hirsch's Frankfort-am-Main. Indeed it could be assumed, and generally was, that there was an inevitable decline from generation to generation in terms of knowledge, conviction and identity. Hence the ultra-Orthodox could well accuse Hirsch, as perhaps they did, of acting as though there were no present danger, as though a pithy statement, a warm smile and the celebration of theological affirmations by leaders and their diminishing flock, meant that all was right with the (Jewish) world.

Hirsch might not have been as forbearing today about the spiritual wanderings of his young student as he was one hundred and fifty years ago. I believe that he was worried and saddened by Graetz' budding secularism. After all, Hirsch did not accept the standard traditionalist line of "don't worry, just do" or "just believe". He may have intuited that the Jewish loyalties and attachments that gave anti-theological positions an aura of piety and innocence were soon to be replaced by a multitude of options in diverse streams of Judaism, in secular Zionism, and in countless narratives strewn about.

41

Hirsch would have liked the humor behind the story of the medieval Jew who, together with a Christian, was commanded by the king of the realm to prove God's existence. The Christian, so the story goes, duly recited the scholastic philosophical proofs for God's existence. But the Jew replied, with seeming innocence, "I am commanded to pray three times a day. Would I pray to someone who doesn't exist?" The neo-Orthodox Hirsch of yesteryear might have smiled and even applauded, but probably no longer believed that such outbursts of playful *hashkafah*, even when delivered with style in flawless German, would suffice in the times already upon him.

And indeed, the seeming tranquility and innocence underlying such stories were bought too cheaply, and do not account for the intellectual and religious life of Jews who live in a wide and open world, with no end of meta-narratives available from East and West and seemingly unbounded experience waiting to be tasted.

Nor do they adequately represent the traditional Jewish world. After all, the reason that every word, every letter, of sacred writings was lovingly interpreted throughout more than two millennia was not *only* in order to glean from them the divine will and word, as from a guide book, and simply to 'do it'. It was also in order to make already acknowledged belief and practice plausible, profound and endearing. In short, interpretation, including much halakhic decision-making, could be said to be about theology. It was expected to make sense, against the backdrop of what the student believed about God and Torah. It was expected to take cognizance of everything else the learner believed and to evaluate this store of knowledge and experience, by virtue of sacred texts, as, respectively, positive or pernicious.

For many years I have taught in the field of Philosophy of Jewish Education. This domain of research, and especially that branch of it entitled Normative Philosophy of Jewish Education, called me to careful and detached study of various visions, ideologies and theologies of Jewish education, as well as analysis of relevant clusters of concepts. Among the differences between philosophy and theology, the cardinal one may be stated as follows: Students and teachers of philosophy are expected to ask basic questions about the world, the nature of knowledge and the value of values with no foregone conclusions or unacknowledged commitments and convictions. Students of theology, on the other hand, speak manifestly from within a tradition that *has* foregone conclusions yet harbors dilemmas, especially when it is challenged, and elicits struggles with complexity from its scholars and saints. They engage in efforts to defend a heritage, even in times of crisis; they spell out its basic assumptions and try to make sense of a life lived within it. That they know this to be difficult and not readily achieved, differentiates them from many 'anti-theological' believers who make do with what we have called *"hashkafah"*, a rehearsed inventory of what is to be believed unquestioningly by those who are loyal.

While my inclinations as an educator are theological for I want parents and teachers to come to grips honestly with the great perennial issues of faith and spiritual and religious life in our time, yet from within a faithful community, my training and my teaching, as university based, are philosophical. This means that I teach, or am supposed to teach, as though my convictions don't matter. This in itself is no small challenge when the discipline being taught is – education. My 'fear' has been that if I express forthrightly what I believe and why, I may find myself no longer welcome in the circle of credible scholars who look askance at classic doctrines and look 'critically' upon those allegedly benighted people who have a stake in them. Conversely, as already noted, I stand to be barred from the circle of religious believers who regard critical sensibility to be sterile, and critical inquiry – heretical.

Regarding the inhibition stemming from the dichotomy between writing critically and yet remaining within a tradition, I now wonder whether it is not based on a mistake, or conceit, that characterizes academic teachers; namely, the sharp contradistinction they often make between philosophy and theology. This, it now seems to me, is largely artificial. I think that theologians know how to distinguish between theology and *hashkafah*. Conversely, it seems to me that we are required to try and see these experiences as part of a whole, no matter how complex the loom of experience. Hence a philosophy of religion or a philosophy of Judaism is barren if it is indifferent to what is actually transpiring in the life of faith, and fails to bring new exegesis to its texts and sacred contexts; if it pays no notice to new problems, patterns of piety and scholarship. At the same time, to delete the discernments of the past undercuts the entire enterprise.

On the other hand, there are seemingly theological approaches that are really *hashkafah* and they may come to view commitment as an excuse to evade untrammeled inquiry and intellectual honesty. In this approach, everything held true is obvious and non-negotiable. "World view" requires no defense and no reflection sparked by the richness of experience. Its main use is to foster loyalty to it; to accept conformity and affirmation.

And yet the *hashkafah* position is not groundless. Dewey and others who deal philosophically with a tradition do not always have in their experience the need to cherish it, and often they do not. And so they do not fully comprehend the theological commitment and trepidation: the commitment that religious thought be a labor of love so that the tradition may continue to live in the hearts and minds of its subjects. And trepidation: because the tradition may disappear, some time in the future, if it is no longer expanded by the wisdom of those who cherish it.

People and Faith

In his well known and intriguing essay, "The Jew in the World,"[2] Martin Buber presents a thesis that has had a great impact on biblical studies, on exegesis, on Zionism and – on theology. He posits that the Jewish people, in its formative years, underwent an overpowering experience that they interpreted as a revelation of God. The outcome of this experience of encounter they understood as a command to constitute themselves both as a community of faith and as a nation, an occurrence that he posits as unique in human history. In Buber's words:

Only in one instance do [religion and nation] coincide. Israel receives its decisive experience *as a people*; it is not the prophet alone but the community as such that is involved. The community of Israel experiences history [i.e., its "national life"] and revelation [i.e., its "religious life"] as one phenomenon, history as revelation and revelation as history. In the hour of its experience of faith the group becomes a people. Only as a people can it hear what it is destined to hear.[3]

Furthermore, a Jewish nation cannot exist without religion any more than a Jewish religious community without nationality.

If we want to be nothing but normal, we shall soon cease to be at all... The great values we have produced issued from the marriage of a people and a faith.[4]

The implications and ramifications of this thesis are wide indeed. Abraham, the harbinger of the nation, now appears as its first prophet. The exodus is a political uprising and subsequent victory, but it is also the framework and context for the giving of the Torah. The land of Israel is a national heritage but also "God's inheritance". Theology, then, describes the relationship between God and the Jewish people. This relationship, in given historical contexts, may appear as a story of religious fervor; at other times, one of anguish and alienation. If there is protracted exile, there is soul searching and penitence; when there is a Jewish commonwealth, prophets may warn and kings or prime ministers celebrate their power and sovereignty. Theology, mediated on this relationship, is not by any account only about religious belief, but also about issues in Jewish life in which God can be said to be present or in which His apparent absence is lamented and even hued by rebellion against his "kingship".

In this book, I discuss six such issues, questions of theology in Jewish life and education. The first concerns itself with the relationship of 'enlightened' Jews to the God they hardly believe in; the second, with Jewish religious faith and initiating young people into it in the modern secular world. The third study brings us to an historical event in which God seems visibly present. We point out that moments of salvation not only bring about a sense, collective as well as personal, of God's presence, but also theological interpretations that may differ radically from one another. From there, my study brings us, thematically though not chronologically, to theological issues associated with the Holocaust. A question that will preoccupy us is whether one dare speak of theology, of the Israel-divine relationship, where that relationship appears to have been severed beyond repair. In the fifth essay, we look for new avenues for such a relationship through exploring the uses and contours of the notion of Peoplehood. In Essay Six, we enter the domain of curriculum in its broadest sense – the curriculum of Jewish life that is transmissible, even as it evokes conversation and controversy. Our focus is on ways of understanding such theological issues as the tension

Michael Rosenak

between universalism and particularism, and I attempt to show that educational discourse has rules of its own and problems unique unto itself.

Let us now begin to explore this discourse.

*   My thanks to Vivienne Burstein for her wise and insightful editing of these essays. Thanks also to my students and colleagues for their invaluable contribution to our regular study group, which has enriched my thinking. Particular thanks to Professor Jonathan Cohen for his generous and masterful Introduction piece. Finally, my thanks to Dr. Zvi Bekerman and Professor Barry Holtz, respectively of the Hebrew University's Melton Centre for Jewish Education and the Jewish Theological Seminary of America, for bringing this volume to publication.

1. See Abraham Joshua Heschel, *God in Search of Man: A Philosophy of Judaism*, New York: Farrar, Straus and Cudahy, 1955, Chapter 32, "Religious Behaviorism", pp. 320-335

2. Martin Buber: "The Jew in the World", in idem, *Israel and the World: Essays in a time of crisis*, New York: Schocken Books, 1948, 2nd edition, 1963, pp. 167-172

3. Ibid. p. 169

4. Martin Buber, "Hebrew Humanism", in Buber, *Israel and the World*, p. 252

I

The Relationship of Enlightened Jews to the God They Hardly Believe In: A Witticism about Modern Jewish Life

A Traditional Tale

I remember being amused and put vaguely at ease by a story I first heard at the age of ten or so. As told to me and to my fellow pupils in 'Hebrew school' the story tells of two Jewish immigrants, an optician from Minsk and a Yiddish school teacher from Pinsk, in early twentieth century New York. Both saw themselves as heretics. One day, the 'Minsker', a one-time 'yeshiva boy', invited himself to spend a Sabbath with the 'Pinsker' whose *apikorsut* (heresy) was legendary. The Pinsker agreed to host him and the Minsker arrived at the home of his host well before the advent of the Sabbath. He lost no time explaining that he hoped, during the course of that Shabbat, to be enriched by insights into free-thinking. The Pinsker greeted him cordially but seemed diffident about engaging in conversation. He just pointed out that there remained less than an hour "to Shabbis" and that they didn't want to be late for the *mikveh* (ritual bath).

The Minsker, a former Hasid, had been taught that one could learn something from every move of the righteous, even from the way they tied their shoelaces! So he dutifully accompanied the Pinsker to the *mikveh* for ritual immersion and then, after candle lighting, to the synagogue for the evening service. The sumptuous family Sabbath meal that followed was accompanied throughout by Sabbath melodies and songs and what seemed quite traditional snippets, as well as mini-sermons by guests and by the host on the weekly Torah reading.

And so it went. Early on the Sabbath morning the host took his perturbed guest to Sabbath services where the latter was honored by an *aliyah*; he was "called up" to the reading of the Torah. This was an awkward moment for the Minsker, since tradition required him to stand at such moments within the congregation and publicly bless God for choosing Israel and for "giving us a Torah of truth". The Minsker, of course, had his doubts on both scores.

These goings on were followed by the midday Sabbath meal and thereafter, a good Sabbath nap. Then came the afternoon prayers, followed by the late afternoon "Third Meal" and finally, *Havdalah*, the ceremony marking the end of the Sabbath. The Minsker's frustration grew at every stage of these surprising happenings. He was indeed too furious to exchange words with his host who seemed gently amused. Before returning to his home early the next morning, he turned to the Pinsker with a bitter complaint: "I came to learn heresy from you and all I got was study and prayer and song. I felt as though I was in the home of a rabbi, not an *apikorus* (heretic)!"And then, an anguished afterthought: "Can it be that you are a *relapsed apikorus*?"

The Pinsker was shocked: "A relapsed *apikorus*? God forbid! But what are you trying to tell me? Do you mean to say that you don't do these things in your home?"

"Of course not! I am an *apikorus!*" To which the Pinsker responded, mockingly, "You are no *apikorus*. You are an *am ha'aretz*! (an ignoramus)."

The Solace of Being Inside a Story

Quite a considerable amount of baggage travels with that story. It expresses a deep-seated bias, prevalent among traditional communities, among 'insiders', against theology. Theology might be useful and suitable for non-Jews who lived by faiths and doctrines that required constant defense and explication. For Jews, among whom actions and not beliefs come first, this was said to be superfluous. Judaism was 'a way of life' which, so it was made to appear, required no reflection. Socialization was what Jewish life and Jewish education were about. *Doing* was the text; *thinking* about it, the often superfluous footnote.

I used to love that story. It celebrated community, loyalty, continuity and shared habit. Yet eventually I became perturbed by it. I understood what its basic thrust was: that there is, or should be, no way out of Jewish commitment and no way to significant change. What the man of Minsk surely saw as a heroic attempt to change something, and to be changed himself, was reduced to an allegedly pathetic, amusing, display of ignorance. That story, I eventually saw, walks hand in hand with the problematic bias that as long as you do what you are supposed to do and what everyone who is anyone does, you can think and believe whatever you wish. Does that mean that Jews are not meant to have conceptions and visions of the fine human being, informed and shaped by Jewish belief and commitment? Are reflective conversation and writings mere banter?

The Minsker was an early twentieth century free-thinker, a non-religious man, a heretic no less. This man had read the great works of the non-believers who called themselves 'enlightened', that is, the people who saw themselves as liberated from religion. He was a child of Judaism, which he had come to reject, and an heir of modernity, science and skepticism, all of which he accepted as self-understood and beneficent. Though reason dictated that he refrain from transmitting the superstitions and tall tales of his Jewish heritage to his own children, yet he sought counsel from a fellow *Jewish* heretic, a fellow *apikorus*, so he thought, with whom he could share his doubts and tribulations; a 'rebbe' from whom he could learn.

Why all this?

He had come to realize that being a true heretic raised many questions. If Jewish belief had spoken to him until his years at the Yeshiva – where he had read agnostic tracts under the table, beneath tomes of Talmud – how could he be sure that his present heretical views were properly grounded? Many questions had turned him away from it all, and tomes of religious scholarship had become dry and scholastic to him. The weight of his experience and thinking had smothered the faith in him – the substantial presence of evil in the world; the silence of God; the manifold sorrows of the people of Israel; the apparent meaninglessness of life…

These were serious issues, and should have sufficed to give his skepticism firm foundations, but the man of Mintz was still perplexed. How had so many wise and profound Jews, people of integrity, lived with these questions without relinquishing their faith? What had been Judaism's teachings on such matters in the past? Was there, hidden within the teachings of the Judaism that he had cast off, a path for him in his contemporary world, a code waiting to be deciphered, even now? This question could be no more than whispered for, in fact, he believed that all his previous beliefs had been rendered false, even ludicrous, by the Enlightenment and its rational faith. Nevertheless, he wanted a profound person to explain it all to him, ordering his troubled mind, helping him to become, once again, a person who walked on the path of truth, even if it was a different one from that of his childhood.

On Second Thought, Is This an Amusing Story?

After growing up and thinking about it, I found the story less comforting and heartwarming than it once had been. True, in adolescence it had strengthened my sense of belonging, of being an insider in Jewish life as it 'really is' and it ridiculed hapless outsiders, who might be reaching for understanding and insight but who could be dismissed simply as pathetic ignoramuses, as *amai ha'aretz*.

What the answer of the Pinsker conveyed was that there was no way out of the tradition short of conversion and taking on alien acts. For, after all, it didn't matter what you thought or believed but only what you did, how you continued to be 'in the know', how you 'practiced Judaism' and remained 'a good Jew'. So the principled refusal of our

'Minsker' to act on the basis of principles in which he did not believe was adroitly shed of significance. He had gone to one he believed to be a wise man looking for guideposts on the tortuous road of modern Jewish life which, after all, was somehow also his: he had not relinquished Jewish identity and had not converted to another faith... He had come looking for profundity but got nothing but a show.

This seemingly heart-warming and identity-building little tale now strikes me as perhaps snide and even mean-spirited. The man we ridiculed in 'Hebrew school', the Minsker, now strikes us as a sincere individual looking for truth and anxious for instruction on how to 'do' it. He intuits that there should be some connection between what we think and how we act, and feels that any system that teaches faithfulness but lacks both faith and integrity cannot endure. He seems indeed the more profound of the two. So how may these two individuals find themselves in a situation of discourse, after all?

Perhaps the problem is with our binary, strictly either-or system of categorization which leads to distortion. On what basis do we condemn the Pinsker? Should we not examine his conception of God and Israel before condemning him for being different from the Minsker and for seeming incoherent in his thoughts and deeds? What kind of theory can help us to clarify the differences and similarities between these two modern Jewish figures? Are we simply looking for ways to dismiss the Pinsker or for a theory that will help us to understand him? And what is true of the Pinsker must also be true of the Minsker. Who is he? When he says 'religion', what does he mean? What is his basic orientation in the world? To help us to address these questions we will turn to the thought of Ernst Akiva Simon,[1] a philosopher of education and Jewish scholar. I shall draw on Simon's thesis and suggest one way of reading it and expanding upon it.

One Thesis on Jewish Religion

I begin with a basic foundation stone of Simon's religious thought: Certain religious cultures, with Judaism prominent among them, have viewed the religious life as all-embracing and comprehensive. In such religious cultures, which he terms "Catholic", nothing is outside the domain of religion. Its teachers and scholars maintain that the needs and obligations of human beings are in essence religious, as is indeed their entire world. The task of people in 'this world' is to actualize the religious demands made on them and to be blessed thereby. Whatever falls outside this religious world is either foolish, or, from the stand-point of a given "Catholic" religion, idolatrous. At best, it is simply trivial. The obligation of every person is to serve God according to his or her ability, through the forms mandated by religion for achieving righteousness and salvation. The Jewish legal, moral and exegetical corpus known as the Oral Torah, with the centrality of the Halakhah within it, is a primary case in point. This corpus, from the perspective of the Talmudic sages and of their spiritual descendants who constitute the historical rabbinic community, has a say in every human activity and pursuit. There are laws of agriculture as well as commerce, of prayer as of marital life. The Halakhah is a religious language that points Jews, in all they do, toward the service of God. The Scriptural declaration, "In all your ways, know Him"[2] reflects the "Catholic" religion ideal. On the basis of the omniscience of the Halakhah, the divinely ordained law, one may say of God that "no place is vacant of Him", for God is present wherever the Halakhah governs human affairs and there is no 'place' that is not of concern to the Halakhah, at least in principle. Therefore the idea that God is always present is transformed into an ideal and perennial aspiration. And to those who know themselves to be in God's presence, there are, as said, no secular activities of significance.

The Move to "Protestantism"

Simon points out that this pan-halakhic ambience is not only at loggerheads with the contemporary ideal of human autonomy but that it also does not adequately describe the classic prophetic vision that too is central in Jewish teaching. It should not be denied that the prophetic vision always lived in proximity to the halakhic one but that, at times, it was in a state of confrontation with its halakhic demands. Yet what both had in common was a vision of life as service of God and love of God. Simon points out that the prophetic ideal turns more to the individual than does the Halakhah which is mostly articulated on a social canvas. This made it possible for religions that stressed, or learned to stress, the individual and his yearnings for transcendence, to make themselves at home in modernity. Those that did so, he calls "Protestant". "Protestants", as he depicts them, are oriented towards the individual, agreeing to place various realms of what came to be known as 'culture' outside of the religious domain and even liberated from it.

But modern culture itself demanded a great deal. Some would say – everything. This culture, in the course of several hundreds of years, overwhelmed and restricted religion and stripped it of its once comprehensive authority in the name of human autonomy. It became confined to given moments, ceremonial occasions, subjective attitudes of conscience and piety and freely chosen forms of communal association that express national or social norms. Thus culture has not only 'liberated' itself from religious norms and demands, but often tailors religion to meet its purposes and needs.

The Move to Secularism

Culture, then, became omnipresent, imbuing all forms of modern consciousness: inquiry, habits and patterns of thought and acceptable action as set forth by modern and social philosophy. This process whereby all we know and believe is explained as a component of culture or an achievement of its secular civilization, is extensive and comprehensive. It now appears to most moderns that religion itself is no more than one department of culture, one that we understand, 'use' and re-fashion for our purposes. Ultimately, it is 'known' to us through the use of the same critical methods of observation and exploration that are current throughout the world of scientific disciplines. Moreover, 'placing' religion among other cultural artifacts,

Michael Rosenak

held like them under the bright lights of the laboratory, exposes to view its apparent weaknesses and fantasies.

This development, of the secularization of human life, is said to accord freedom of thought and action. Yet religion seems to have been prematurely transported to the archives of archaic culture. For even as the alleged demise of "Catholic" religion created an exhilarating consciousness of freedom, it did not totally devastate the religious sensibilities of believers. The 'explainable' character and transitory nature of what we thought we knew as perennial and sacred, absolutely created a heady consciousness of adventure in those who defined themselves as secular. Yet in others it fostered a sense of abandonment to be borne and a task to be undertaken.

Faiths: "Catholic", "Protestant" and Secular World Views

The sense of abandonment characterized "Catholics" who asked why God had deserted or so drastically tested then, but who still dared to anticipate the restored glory of "Catholic religion". The sense of 'a task to be undertaken' distinguished "Protestants" who joined the world of culture, but with an important stipulation: namely, that they be accepted on their own terms, as people who maintain a separate and essential compartment of their lives as irreducibly religious. They joined the forces of modernity and played various roles in the life of culture but often insisted that they had the religious right and duty to mend the (secular) world by bringing transcendence and prophetic judgment into its public domain. Some, more quietist, looked to the mending of the modern situation by religious testimony and lives of piety wherein they found guidelines for building the individual and his and her spirituality. Among the latter, sources of religion were re-examined from a "Protestant" perspective and were found to be rich in existential teachings which, even in an age termed "post-modern", spoke in particular to the person in search of adequate 'narratives' by which to live.

Here, then, is the point of origin of "Protestant" religion. The "Protestant" partakes of culture and joins it, the better to infuse it with a religious spirit where possible, and in order to judge it where necessary. So she or he not only participates but also stands outside it, and judges it, frequently from new post-modern perspectives.

"Catholic religions", as a type, find this modern yet pious (outsider-insider) approach thorny. It has a modern sophistication about it, of living in two worlds as valuative positions that, in principle, may seem inauthentic to "Catholics". Where "Catholic religiosity" remains a live option, its normative adherents do not quite share an overarching conception of culture with modern secularism and thus are readily dismissed by the "non-Catholics" as primitive or archaic. Since, in principle, they do not suffer limits placed on religion's (i.e., God's) sovereignty, they can be handily dismissed as enemies of freedom.

To summarize: The world of all-embracing culture is intent on leaving no space free for religion at all except for that religion which is a constituent and a confidant of culture – and is in its service. For the truly secular society cannot countenance religion independent of culture, standing outside it and judging it in the name of transcendence.

People whose spiritual inclination is towards "Catholicism" appear ultimately to have three choices: they can remain "Catholic", and pay the price for it; they can become "Protestants" who have joined culture but subtly, somewhat on their own terms; and they may reject religion in the name of secularism that has shaken off the yoke of belief and tradition and has built "Catholic", that is, comprehensive social and cognitive structures, of its own.

A possible option, and one perhaps ultimately unavoidable on the part of consistent "Catholics", is to segregate themselves to some degree, maintaining within the enclaves in which they choose to live a kind of "Catholic universe". But to the outsider, the "Catholicism" of segregated groups appears ineffectual and even escapist – and illusionary. After all, this all-inclusive conception wherein "Catholicism" claims to remain a total experience obviously incorporates a smaller proportion of what there actually *is* in the world than used to be the case! It cannot be said to encompass all reality as that term was previously understood. This approach, then, redefines all of 'reality', and limits its scope to that which can be maintained, protected and supervised within a strict normative community. To outsiders this community appears sectarian, but to its adherents it is the very embodiment of a 'world' still in place by virtue of a righteous remnant. This group awaits the day of the restored reign of ("Catholic") religion. In the case of consistent and strict "Catholics", all spiritual infiltration is to be kept at a distance for, in the eyes of the faithful community and its leaders, they are based on principles that are profoundly mistaken and often dangerous. Writing in the early 1950s, Simon mentions the *Neturai Karta* ultra Orthodox Jerusalem-based group as an example of a "Catholic religious community". It should be noted, however, that since the days of Simon's monograph, *most* ultra-Orthodox communities share in the segregationist ambience to some degree. Indeed, it can be stated that in the secular world, one cannot remain a "Catholic" without (some) segregation.

However the mainstream response to the attack on religion is non-segregationist and "Protestant". "Protestants" are members (whether by circumstance not actively resisted, or by conviction) of the community of culture carrying the impress of the secular world. They may regret the overwhelming influence of secularism on society, but they come to terms with it for their own reasons: mainly, that they see themselves as having a task within it. As said, they represent religious transcendence that judges as well as participates. So, they are closely tied to culture for they are always on hand to point to society's corruption and to religion's ability to redeem it. But "Protestants" speak the language of culture in which they feel at home, despite theological reservations. They may and do engage in all professions; conversation on any subject is possible with them. They differ from others in the modern world insofar as they are indisputably religious people. Often the ground of their religiosity is a desire to salvage what can be restored or maintained from once regnant "Catholic" ages and faiths. Those of this sensibility often define themselves as classicists, as value-driven people; others may see them as reactionaries. However, they generally view themselves as 'rescuing religion' by making room for it as an independent entity alongside yet above the secular world.

"Protestants" draw a clear line of demarcation between religion and 'culture', between the holy and the profane. This form of religion cultivates its limited authority. It is much concerned with theology. It sees its roots in religiously-oriented humanism and/or transcendence; it bears the Word of God. In Judaism, "Protestant" religion is focused on the prophets of Israel; its thrust is "fear of Heaven", a pious sensibility. Its institutions of education wish to foster individuals who have qualities of inwardness, people who can pray, who have, in Simon's words, "a second innocence". At times, individual "Protestants" succumb to the spirit of the age and become secular; at other times, they become fanatical believers who feel commanded to transmit the fire of religious passion to the sinful. For many "Protestants", however, religion is an orientation to life, a way of grappling with the world of holiness, a pious, sometimes lyrical, sometimes sentimental way of being a human being.

Because of its strongly "Catholic" character, embodied in the all-encompassing and authoritative Halakhah, Judaism has had particular difficulties in adjusting to modernity and the omnipresence of secular culture, says Simon. Many Jews who are generally identified as liberal have, in the modern world, sought justification for "Jewish Protestant religion". They have portrayed Judaism as enlisting 'the heart', and as grappling with existential problems. They have emphasized texts of Judaism that allow for a more "Protestant" reading of the tradition, such as Genesis, Jonah, Job, Psalms, as well as midrashic teachings and Hasidic tales. These have been emphasized in Jewish teaching for they are said to bring into view the inner light of Judaism and its concern with the individual, with his and her quest for a secure home for meaning, as well as pivotal subjects like *Tikkun Olam* (repairing the world), the educated person, and the quest for atonement.

These approaches have drawn much attention in groups of seekers and existentialists and coteries of individuals who have chosen to see Judaism and its innovative communities as the address for spiritual and religious creativity and development within and through the Jewish tradition. There is a new emphasis on Hasidic music in prayer, a new interest in Jewish mysticism, the study of non-halakhic Jewish texts, and the creation of more intimate communities that are seen to address the needs of congregants rather to spell out their alleged communal obligations.

Yet, as Simon points out, such "Protestant Judaism" has had great difficulty in making itself credible, in contradistinction to other traditions, eastern and western. The primacy of Halakhah is so ensconced in Judaism that attempts to give it a "Protestant" shape and image frequently convey an impression of assimilation and inauthenticity, of non-seriousness and ignorance. "Protestant religion" is always in search of theology; yet in the Jewish tradition, even when it is presented as "Protestant", theology is not prominent. "Catholicism", encompassing all, does not enjoy arguing for its place under the sun. Hence, continues Simon, the Protestant Christian may look 'more religious' than the Catholic one; he can draw on venerable theological sources within his tradition. He does not, as Jewish would-be "Protestants" frequently do, appear both clerical and alien.

Coming back to the Pinsker heretic, his Judaism is unabashedly "Catholic", for "Catholicism" is, after all, the real article. But he often forgets to mention and sometimes does not understand that his seemingly comprehensive Jewish life is itself in the service of a culture which is all-embracing, and hence decidedly "Catholic", of course now in a new, secular, manner. He has jettisoned the normative beliefs that underlie the practice that he continues to maintain 'religiously'! This "secular Catholicism" seeks to displace the Judaism he cherishes.

Four Options for Contemporary Jewish Life

Four options suggest themselves to me from Simon's model: (a) ultra-Orthodoxy; (b) cultural Zionism; (c) secular-oriented compartmentalization, and (d) Modern Orthodoxy.

The ultra-Orthodox community claims to understand the situation most straightforwardly. It continues to live in an unambiguously "Catholic" ambience which, to its mind, is the only 'authentic' one. Everything (as far as is possible in 'exile' under the rule of Gentiles or of secular Zionist Jews in Israel) is conducted in tightly knit communities that claim to live by the Halakhah; all are subservient to religious authorities who rule on all fields of activity.

"Protestant" religion is declared foreign, 'goyish'. But for this "Catholicism" to survive in the secular world, it must build a social structure that is thoroughly committed to self segregation. Paradoxically, the seemingly 'all encompassing world' these "Catholics" create is narrow. As for the world of culture outside the community, it is judged to be evil, empty of values. It is to be held at arms length and shut out except with regard to those realms in which contact is deemed necessary for survival, or where interchange is grudgingly ruled to be harmless or neutral.

On the other hand, cultural Zionists have sought to transform Jewish culture itself. They perceive it as a collective Jewish task to create a new, secularized, "Catholic" world view and way of life that still, in many ways, looks like a religion and which can be said to be singularly Jewish. This conceptual construction becomes plausible in the light of Judaism's blending of religious and national characteristics. The American Jewish thinker, Mordecai Kaplan, is a prime example of a Jewish leader who insists that Jewish religion is part of Jewish civilization (i.e., culture) but he accepts that this is only one of the two cultures ('civilizations') in which Jews live. Thus we have here a blending of secularized but unmistakably Jewish "Catholicism" and religiously-tinged secularism.

Liberal Jews in the Diaspora and in Israel, as well as political Zionist thinkers, have taken a third approach, namely a secular-oriented compartmentalization. They have consciously accepted the modern model: They live in a secular world in which religion is either dismissed or assigned a particular and circumscribed cultural role.

The pithy sentiment of Theodore Herzl, "we shall keep our priests within the confines of their temples in the same way as we shall keep our professional army within the confines of their barracks,"[3] well expresses both the compartmentalized status of religion as serving a kind of social role and a sometimes hidden secular contempt for religion. Their identity as citizens in the modern world of secularism is unequivocal and experienced as liberating.

The Intriguing Sociology of Modern Orthodoxy[4]

Taking Simon one step further, it seems to me that the difficulties encountered by "Protestant" religion within the confines of a Judaism that is, in principle, incorrigibly "Catholic", is best embodied by that community of Jews who are termed "Modern Orthodox". Modern Orthodox Jews hold to a "Catholic"-type view of Judaism and believe that it remains genuine only when practiced as such. Moreover it is this "Catholic Judaism" that they cherish. They, like the ultra-Orthodox, profess that they await the day when Judaism will be restored to its pristine "Catholic" character, 'as in the days of yore'. At the same time, they are opposed to self segregation which shuts out the alien 'world'; hence they share with all other non-segregationist religious publics, a "Protestant orientation". They will insist that Judaism remains "Catholic" but admit that this orientation is in historical eclipse, to be restored only in Messianic times. As a result, Modern Orthodox Jews who are religious Zionists, whether in Israel or the Diaspora, often tend to messianic ideology which points the way, through Zionism, to a rebirth of "Catholic Judaism". Yet the modern sensibility they share with all modern (i.e., "non-Catholic") religionists deeply affects and even transfigures this vision. For, in fact, those ideological "Catholics" create a "Protestant" culture of their own, like all moderns who would be religious but look askance at segregation. Why so?

We may recall: Like all "Protestants", Modern Orthodox Jews are members of the secular society. They speak like their neighbors, in a language nuanced by general culture, influenced by fads. They are at home in the world of commerce and have mastered academic discourse. If they are members of the middle class, we may expect them to travel widely much like others of their social class. However, while doing so, they remain loyal to the "Catholic" norms and prohibitions of the Halakhah even while touring the world. Thus, males are careful to don *tephillin* every morning and all observe the laws associated with Sabbath rest and with halakhic dietary restrictions (*kashrut*). And we may expect conscientious persons to devote some time each day to Torah study.

And, I would ask, why then all the bother? Why not stay at home, in the natural habitat of halakhic life? Clearly, for those Modern Orthodox Jews who wish to share in modern secular culture and hence to go on vacations, the "Catholic Halakhah" can be heard advising to get back home from wherever they have gone for their 'recreation', before the advent of the Sabbath. Or, they may stay with halakhically-observant friends or relatives, or be in Israel or elsewhere at an observant and kosher facility. If all this is unfeasible and does not fit in with their vacation plans, they will bring canned foods with them, to be eaten in the awkward privacy of their hotel rooms. Or, happily, they will find a kosher restaurant where, at exorbitant prices they may eat kosher food, *as though* they were home, *as though* they weren't really on vacation at all. *As though* they didn't have the headache of electronic hotel-room keys which on Shabbat, according to the Halakhah, prevent free access to the rooms they have rented. This behavior, so strange in the eyes of their Gentile or non-observant Jewish travel companions, is perceived by them as a heroic gesture of piety, as a declaration that what they have done keeps the religious option of life afloat without requiring its adherents to live in self-segregation! Stated less prosaically and more existentially, they have kept faith with their religion; they have borne witness, albeit as "Protestants", to the truth of the "Catholic Torah". Though within culture, Modern Orthodoxy remains a judge of culture. It is an existential "Protestantism" built on the foundations of an historical "Catholicism".

Once Again: The 'Pinsker' and the 'Minsker'

In terms of my expansion of Simon's model, we can try to place our two heretical gentlemen. Both of them live in a world which proclaims a kind of "Catholicism" of its own: the all-encompassing rule of secular culture and its divinities that nourish desires and facilitate achievements. The Pinsker accepts this as positive; after all, the secular society makes room for him and assures him the free right to live within his own sub-culture. This is a function of the freedom secular democracy bestows on the individual in his associations as in his solitude. But the Pinsker seems oblivious to the sociology of the situation: how long will his cognitively deviant Jewish culture appear valuable and convincing to him when everyone round-about is doing other things? Can it be transmitted intact to coming generations? It would seem that only a vibrant "Protestantism" can achieve this goal, but that is definitely not on the Pinsker's agenda. He is not religious and feels stifled in "Protestant" communities which seem self-consciously to wear religion on their sleeves, even when these impress him for their dedication. He can join them, but never out of conviction. As for contemporary "Catholic" ones: he will surely suffocate in a community that persecutes non-believers and flouts its own, to him, narrow "Catholicism" as though it were 'the world'. Nor is he a candidate for membership in their community of self-segregation. After all, he is a heretic!

As for secular-oriented compartmentalism, it appears to him as just another form of assimilation: he has little patience with 'Hebrew speaking goyim'. So, willy-nilly, he finds himself in the camp of cultural Zionists who translate the language of tradition into the language of secular culture. But there is room for him to be perturbed for the survival of *Yiddishkeit* in this secular "Catholic" ambience. After all, he, unlike the political thinkers of political Zionism, lives in the consciousness that the Jews have been a faith as well as a people. He seems oblivious to the likelihood that future generations of Jews, educated in the Ahad Ha'am orientation, will themselves become uninterested in maintaining Jewish forms of cultural life. As said, there is too much going on out there. In fact there are too many identities to choose from or, more precisely, to partake of. There are too many narratives.

What about the Minsker? Will he remain a "Catholic secularist", leaving religion but also "(Catholic) Jewish nationality" behind him? It seems unlikely. He takes the issue of heresy, the flip side of faith, too seriously. I venture that he may eventually find himself in Jewish or non-Jewish communities which dwell on holiness, spirituality and other expressions of "Protestant" religion, in Judaism or outside of it. Perhaps he will find a home in Reform or Conservative movements of Jewish renewal to which he brings his background of taking seriously 'the large questions'; an outlook to which "Protestants" are much inclined. Or, perhaps, he will find himself within ultra-Orthodoxy, as one who has come to the truth. Finally, he may turn to Modern Orthodoxy. There his willingness to abandon his heretical past will be appreciated as commendable and courageous, and he himself will view his Orthodoxy as the solution to a crisis of faith. He will be respected in that community, so "Catholic", yet, from his perspective, so "Protestant", even if he is not always quite 'figured out'.

We remain with a central problem, much discussed above but as yet unresolved, more perturbing for "Protestants" than "Catholics"; namely, why does the Pinsker claim to dislike a Judaism of 'thought' while he seems respectful and even strangely committed to Jewish acts?

True, he can cite chapter and verse about Jewish culture's preference for deeds. But then, why does he engage in 'thought' as well, as we have observed him doing? After all, at his Sabbath table there are *divrai Torah*. We may conjecture that these include "words of Torah" generally related to the 'Portion of the Week', words of Midrash, even some philosophy and medieval commentary. It is true, as we have already remarked, that even a man like the Pinsker understands that action rests on a structure of ideas which organize that action, give it a context and make sense of it. So what is it that he cannot abide in the Minsker? Why does he polemically dismiss him, calling him an *am ha-aretz* for his failure to understand Judaism as *doing?* Why does the Minsker's search for true ideas about religion and the Jewish people and God and commandments render his desire for the truth – however "Protestant" and assimilationist this may be in the eyes of the Pinsker – unworthy of response? The incongruity of this (non-)conversation is such that he, the Minsker, suspects the Pinsker of a clandestine return to piety!

In suggesting an answer to this question, we may differentiate between three kinds of dealing with ideas, all of which may, in various senses, be understood as "words of Torah." The first, midrashic, or drashic (homiletic) approach, holds that to be occupied by words of Torah is an integral part of the tradition of Torah. One may cite a commentary of Rashi on Genesis that speaks of God's gift of Eretz Yisrael to His people,[5] or a midrash on the desire of the moon to be greater than the sun, (thus punished by becoming smaller)[6] as examples of what the literature of

Torah is engaged in: it inculcates moral attitudes, it makes difficult passages comprehensible, it lays additional layers of complexity on the foundations of Scripture, often to edify but also to celebrate complexity and profundity. Sometimes they are explicit *explications* of Torah, ('here's what it says'); at other times, *justifications* of it ('here is how we may understand it and live with it').

Explication and Justification

I shall briefly expand on the distinction I am making between them. *Explication* teaches us what the text 'is saying'. What it is saying is not always clear, especially to the thinly educated; therefore it must be explained. This often involves having the teacher expose to view 'the true meanings of the text'.

The Pinsker loves Midrash for it demonstrates how the tradition works, how problematic situations are made to come out all right. *Justification* constitutes the answers that have been given to moral or other difficulties in the text. For the dedicated devotees of the text, justifications that arise out of questions and perplexities often appear as explications ('Here is what it means'). Hence "an eye for an eye" will, for some, obviously and eternally means monetary compensation, for God would not have given unjust or cruel laws to the children of His covenant. For others, it will be the consequence of midrashic deliberation which raises the question, 'What should it mean?'.

The Pinsker appreciates both orientations though in his philosophical moments he thinks of most explications as justifications, for he sees the tradition itself as ongoing justification. In any case, both smack of *Yiddishkeit*, both are Torah, to be relished even where they appear unbelievable or outdated. He enjoys *darshanut* for it is a sophisticated way of moving all justifications into explications. The teacher in this model of teaching ideas, 'midrashizes' before the text is permitted to speak. Justification, then, is made to appear as explication. Thus we can expect the teacher in this model to explain the difficult text as 'obviously' meaning what patently it does not 'at first glance' appear to be saying. Such a *drash* may begin with such phrases as "The Torah teaches," followed by an exposition of the essence of Judaism. The Pinsker, as said, appreciates such discourse though, as a heretic, he doesn't believe it. And yet he has no difficulties with statements such as "This is what [this] means and this is the way to see it". Since the authority behind such statements no longer binds him, he can – as a lapsed but strongly identified "Catholic" – simply enjoy them. He has no problem with the way the midrashic mode makes sense of the commandments, and of Jewish experience as a whole. It may be naïve but it is heartwarming to the Pinsker that in the homiletic discourse that he hears at his Sabbath table all matters come out smoothly resolved. When asked whether some of this discourse does not seem ridiculous to him, he smiles.

A second way of treating Judaism as 'Thought' is philosophical: Here we find Judaic scholars, whether in Philosophy, Bible or other related disciplines, laying out what the corpus of Judaism has been found to 'say' on the basis of explorations into these disciplines. With this as well the Pinsker has no problem. Objective study of the Jewish past, systematizing our knowledge of it, is not that world of ideas and beliefs that puts him off. After all the very knowledge that philosophy deals with had a hand in shaping his heretical views. To get from Maimonides to Spinoza, so it seems to him, one walks on one and the same road.

I venture to say that what *does* irritate and anger the Pinsker is the giving of philosophical answers – dealing with ultimate values and making truth claims – to questions that belong to a different, midrashic, universe of discourse. The upshot is that his heresy consists of not taking the Jewish universe of meaning to be a source of reliable knowledge about reality. This is paradoxical given his fervent "Catholic" observance of Jewish practice.

Here we must return to the sorely neglected Minsker. We recall that he traveled a great distance on his pilgrim's journey to learn the foundations of heresy. He was looking for the truth of the views that all "Jewish Catholics" in his surroundings considered mistaken and wicked. He wanted to explore *apikorsut* with a man who had thought deeply upon it. His basic questions were: If the tradition that you live by and love more than I is false, how do we know what to do, how to act? Is there a way to understand divinity and its alleged relationship to human beings in the face of the evil in the world? Is there any sense in which the Torah can still be holy and even "given" to us after we have engaged in 'higher' biblical research? Are you such a fervent "Catholic", even though you are a 'non-believer', because you fear to ask the questions that "Protestants" ask?

What characterizes all these questions is that *drash* is not enough to answer them, and Jewish Thought by itself, is too detached to educate. And here the fundamental questions are, Can I know what Judaism may mean for me? Can I be philosophical but committed too? What is required of those who seek meaning, and what do they do with fragmentary answers? What is the nature of second innocence?

These are questions posed by theology with the fervor of *drash* but with the methodology of philosophy. Theologians cannot promise that 'it will all come together in the end' but their motivation for exploring the issues is religious; it speaks from within the parameters of faith. It hopes and prays that the answers discovered will justify the raising of the questions. But in any case, theologians prefer uncertainties faced squarely to certainties that blur and distort.

It is this that the Pinker dislikes. His intellectual and spiritual life is geared to the modern situation; he does not expect Jewish learning to have the tools and the energies to address problems and, perhaps, to change the way we think. From a theological perspective, it is this that makes him a heretic!

The Minsker is ready to re-examine whether Judaism suggests roads and ways to orient himself towards the focal questions addressed to us by life. That is why he came looking for a 'rebbe'. Although not received kindly by the Pinsker, his precarious journey does depend in large measure on inspiring teachers, including theological exegetes who wish to ask questions of the third, theological

Michael Rosenak

type; those who testify that Judaism is a source for answers, even when incomplete. They are waiting for the next page, the next master, the next question.

1. Ernst Akiva Simon, "Are we Israelis still Jews? The search for Judaism in the new society", in Arthur A. Cohen (ed.) *Arguments and Contexts: A Reader of Jewish Thinking in the Aftermath of the Holocaust*, New York, Evanton and London: Harper and Row, 1970, pp. 388-401

2. Proverbs 3:6

3. Theodore Herzl, *Der Judenstaat (The Jewish State)*, trans. from the German by Sylvie D'Avigdor, 1946, American Zionist Emergency Council, Chapter 4, "Theocracy".

4. The discussion below is a prototype and does not necessarily apply fully to all those who are termed 'Modern Orthodox'.

5. Rashi, Genesis 1:1

6. B.T., Hullin 60B

II

'Translation' and Authenticity in Jewish Learning: Rehabilitating Transcendence

I begin with two episodes that point to the contours of our discussion. In both our episodes, teachers are explaining biblical texts to their pupils. Both have the best intentions and outstanding skills; both are fine teachers of their 'subject matter'. They both feel that it is necessary to translate certain concepts into a relevant 'language' (or symbolic universe) without which the text will not be understood. They are looking for a way of expressing sublime yet, to their students, somehow odd matters; that is, matters they think are outside the realm of children's experience. They offer explanations in the language of the larger culture in which they and their pupils live and think, but in so 'translating', they place communicability as their main aim, rather than authenticity. Wishing to 'translate' the tradition into terms 'kids can understand', they sometimes over-translate. Moved by the worthy cause of relevance in seeking to clarify issues, they lose the transcendence that exposes to view a different perspective. To use Heschel's pithy example, they substitute "Turn on the light" for "Let there be light".

Michael Rosenak

Excising Transcendence

The two episodes I will recount illuminate an educational dilemma in which this issue of translation looms large. Here is the background of the first episode and its story:

In the early years of the State of Israel, many tens of thousands of new immigrants arrived in the country, the vast majority of them from Islamic countries. For the most part, these Jews lived by cultural norms and religious sensibilities that were substantially different from those current among the ruling secular public in Israel which desired, outspokenly and at times callously, to convert the immigrants (*olim*) to their own 'free-thinking' doctrines. These new *olim* also had very different orientations from the national-religious (Modern Orthodox) Zionist old-timers who, though committed to tradition, shared many ideological positions with the secular Zionist public, e.g., the importance in contemporary Jewish life of national 'rebirth' and Hebraic culture. The national-religious Zionists, mostly of European origin, had long been exposed to the cultural language of their non-Jewish environments and had, in varying degrees, learned to accommodate themselves to modern thought and education. These Western Europeans were often firm believers in the principle of *Torah im Derech Eretz* (Torah imbued with worldly culture) as propagated by Rabbi Samson Raphael Hirsch, the nineteenth century founder of neo-Orthodoxy. They acknowledged secular thought and in some measure adopted secular conceptions. At the same time they also built firm ideological defenses against some of its manifestations. These Western European Jews, many of whom held significant positions in the educational enterprise in the public religious sector of the young State of Israel by virtue of their European education, tended to explain too much: what they were doing and what they meant by doing things in this or that particular way, as well as how the tradition should be understood and practiced in its renewed homeland. They revered Judaism and loved the new emphasis on Bible teaching, even though it was imported from the non-Orthodox educational sector as a reaction to traditional Talmudic study (which was said to be 'exilic' and irrelevant). But they also saw their task as bringing children to religious devotion and halakhic practice.

As students of Education, several friends and I had been allowed to sit in on some lessons in Jewish studies in the "National-Religious" (Orthodox-Zionist) school we were visiting on a 'pedagogic tour' in a recently-settled development town. By good fortune, I found myself in the class of a young teacher who was known to be a bright light in the educational firmament; one could sense immediately that the man was unmistakably a teacher, and, albeit a native born Sabra,[1] also unmistakably a *yekke*, (a German Jew).

In this particular lesson, the teacher was dealing with the biblical story of Saul and David.[2] He explained how David's dazzling military successes in the war against the Philistines and the acclaim he received from the people aroused envy and anger in Saul. The teacher pointed to a verse in the Saul-David saga as evidence of this distress. The verse related that "the spirit of God departed from Saul". He explained these words as meaning, "he suffered from what we today call 'clinical depression'. He could not function;

he was in the grips of deep melancholia." Although perhaps surprised that their *'dati'* (religious) teacher could so facilely explain this passage without any reference to God, some of the pupils nodded their heads in a gesture of recognition and illumination. *So that's what it means! Now I understand. I can live with that!* They silently congratulated their teacher for choosing a plausible manner of explaining the text and making it lucid. The grateful pupils had ostensibly learned that, when confronted with 'superstitious' or old-fashioned understanding of the Bible and of God, one might counter with an explanation in the language in which the 'moderns' who ran the state could accept.

Yet one young girl, quite obviously from a non-European family, expressed reservations: *"But why do you call Saul's problem melancholy? The Bible says exactly what his problem was: God's spirit had departed from him."*

In response the teacher was kind but mildly condescending. "I am just explaining what those words, 'God's spirit departed', can mean to the reader of today; what explanations help him 'get the picture'." The pupil remained adamant. *"But Sir, everyone knows what it means. It happens at some time to everyone. Who has not had this experience – of God leaving him?"*

Here the dialogue ended.

In theological terms, my second episode is strikingly similar to the first though it concerns a different public and a different context. Here the pupils were native Israelis and their teacher was a secularist, not as in the first story, an 'enlightened' Orthodox Jew. Here are my notes on the occasion:

My students and I are visiting a secular Jewish high school in the Haifa area. The teacher, a forceful and dramatic man, is teaching Ezekiel's Chapter 15, the prophecy of the "dry bones" that represent the entire House of Israel, to be resurrected, says the prophet, in a time to come. The teacher, I have been told, was educated in an ultra-Orthodox and anti-Zionist community in old Jerusalem, had rebelled against his environment and is now a secular teacher of Bible.

I listen carefully. He presents Ezekiel's prophecy as a stirring call for hope. The dry bones of the people of Israel will again be joined together. The teacher, speaking against the backdrop of the Carmel mountains just outside the window, is impressive and inspiring. Ezekiel, through the teacher's reading, appears to impart a new spirit into his hearers, here-and-now as then. He explains the chapter as an effort by the prophet to do what a fine social worker does when he feels called upon to raise the morale of his client; what a good psychologist does when fighting somber and self-destructive inclinations in a patient.

One pupil in the first row who has been listening carefully and with some excitement, occasionally looking out of the window at the Carmel and the sea where Ezekiel's words could be seen to be coming true, demurs. *"But Meir,"* says the boy, (using the informal first name manner of address customary here), *"why do you say that the prophet is morale building? The Bible says straightforwardly why Ezekiel speaks as he does – 'The hand of God was upon me'. What are we to understand by this? Is there any way we can know what 'God's hand upon him' meant to the prophet when it happened? If we believe the Bible that it did actually happen! The Bible mentions nothing of psychologists or social workers. If that's all this is about, well, we don't need the Bible for that!"*

The teacher's response is self-assured, somewhat amused but brusque. "When they said 'God' they meant the human spirit. That's the way people talked in ancient times." The pupil listens attentively, then drops the subject. Perhaps he has decided that the teacher is "not serious", alienated from the language and experience in which the Bible conveyed its message, or he might have decided that the teacher speaks with the authority of a modern and learned scholar whose view of the Bible was to be trusted.

What characterizes both episodes is that the educator is conveying a sense of what modern discourse 'makes' of God, while each of our two pupils takes issue with this modern rhetoric, sometimes inchoately. They think, or would like to believe, that reading the Torah is an entrance to another world of meaning. This world of meaning cannot be contained in the language of contemporary social science into which the teachers are translating. Both teachers, albeit in different ways, represent the rational world; both have studied the subject matter of the classes they are teaching with the tools of scientific research. What they teach is designed not for future experts or academic researchers, but for children who will hopefully live their lives in a

Jewish culture and should be helped to do so competently, morally, and with a modicum of pleasure. It is assumed that their study of the Bible and Jewish texts, presented as foundational, will shape their identities. It will make them more grounded Jews.

The Bible teacher from the development town in the first episode appears to believe that a way of simplifying the biblical text is to translate it into a language with which all are familiar, with which all have experience. He believes that his translation will bring learners closer to the text by demystifying it; he believes that he must elucidate the text in the direction of modern consciousness, and aim modern consciousness in the direction of the text. Very possibly, as a young Orthodox scholar and a modern religious Zionist Jew, he wishes to impart to his students an understanding that will still allow them to 'own' the text and to recognize it as part of their world. He is in a sense relating how he himself does this in his own life; a life he sees as resting on diverse insights, patterns of thought, and the courage of his convictions. He believes he is bringing the Bible and the God of the Bible to his pupils in a way that they can grasp. But for this, as his pupil intimated, he is paying a price. Substituting another language for that of the Bible means adopting, at least in part, an extraneous paradigm with its own pictures and its own model of reality. In this new scheme of things, the biblical world picture may well become secondary.

As for the Haifa boy in the second episode, he too is taken aback by the assumed common identity between prophets who experienced "the hand of God upon them" and the clients of social workers who are patted on the back and encouraged. Can that be all the Bible is saying? Note: the boy is not attempting to protect tradition, as is the girl in the development town. In the Israeli scheme of things, he is "secular". But he is moved to read this strange text and locate its code before deciphering it. He thinks there may be something important there for him.

'Translation' and its Limits

When might such translation, the substitution of a different frame of reference, appear justifiable or even essential, and when not? I shall note two answers to that question that carry philosophical-educational weight.

1 – *The translation might be said to be necessary because it is grounded in truth claims.* Thus it could be argued that our scholarly knowledge of religious texts and our experiences proscribe taking these texts at face value; we are precluded from regarding them as factual in any conventional way. The teacher who 'translates' on the basis of truth claims will, in such a case, explain, as did our Haifa teacher, that the only way to understand the text is to re-order the way ancient people understood the world and themselves within it, and to explain what they presumably would have said and believed if they had known what we know – i.e., 'updating' the moral frame of reference of the texts.

2 – *Translation may be necessary on pedagogical grounds.* Our teacher, as scholar or as religious believer, may have no fundamental problem with the text in itself and its universe. This may be for one of two reasons. First: it may be that she

distinguishes between the world of the text and her own world, which bears its own normative commitments. Thus she can view the text as historical. In this case, the Bible or any aspect of tradition can make no normative claims on us: it is our history of which we are (usually) not ashamed, but it does not command us. It tells us a good deal about who we are and what we have been, but it cannot tell us what *to be*. The pedagogical translation required is simply a tool that helps learners grasp the Bible in a way that reflects their stage of maturity, that corresponds to issues in their world, and raises questions that are grounded in the text but are not necessarily or explicitly within it. For example there are moral issues that may not have perturbed the biblical writer but do, in our generation, trouble us. Conversely, study of Scripture may spark valuative discussion and raise dilemmas that face not only the contemporary reader, but can often be seen to have troubled the biblical writer as well.

A second motivation for pedagogical translation is that the teacher is searching for ways to build a world-view for and with her pupils by way of the specific subject matter being presented. Indeed, we may expect, or hope, that she has her own theology that is rooted in everything she knows and believes, and that this 'everything' is constantly nourished by new knowledge and experience. It is built on foundations of religious sensibility, of modern science, of culture and of a desire for continuity. Her interpretations of religious sources and her experiences are themselves a translation, but they are a translation continually challenged by the demand for caution and reverence and honesty. It reaches for wholeness and harmony.

This teacher is a philosopher who is pedagogically challenged. She cannot make herself understood except by simplifying, by making the language which she speaks, say in study of Bible or Talmud, comprehensible to children. In contradiction to what she would teach doctoral students in the 'field', and/or, conversely, what she discusses with her friends and colleagues or what she talks about with masters of traditional Torah learning, in the classroom she brackets some of what she knows and values. She sacrifices some knowledge – so that she will be understood. Yet, she must continually ask: When is pedagogical simplification a legitimate or necessary option? When does it advance the education of the young and when is it an act of distortion, denying them the knowledge that can genuinely surprise them and give shape and direction to their experience?

'Translation' Unbounded

I shall illustrate the problems of translation by discussing one writer, the twentieth century scholar and educator, Shlomo Dov Goitein, who espoused translation on cognitive, educational, moral and theological grounds.

In describing his personal development, as a Jew and a teacher, Goitein tells us of his estrangement from Orthodox circles in Frankfort-am-Main where he lived as a youngster and then as student. On the verse from Numbers 15[3] incorporated into the *Kol Nidrai* prayer "and may the transgressions of the entire community of Israel and that of the stranger who dwells in their midst be forgiven," he says, wryly, "'the stranger in their midst' – that's him [i.e., me]!"

But Goitein also describes as formative his Talmud lessons, under the tutelage of Rabbi Nehemia Nobel, the liberal Orthodox sage of Frankfort. He calls Nobel an important mentor; he is a man to whom he refers as his "rabbi".[4]

Goitein went on to become a major scholar of Jewish life in the Moslem world, of Hebrew, History, and Education. He was, for a number of years, supervisor of curriculum in the Israeli Ministry of Education, and he was a teacher. He was also a professor at the Hebrew University and later carried on his Genizah studies at the University of Pennsylvania and at Princeton.

In a book on education,[5] he describes the difficulty young people, as well as older ones, have with the central figure of the Bible: God. Living after Descartes, Kant and Freud, they have come to believe, whether through purposeful inquiry or by osmosis, that modern people have a different conception of 'spirit' than that of the pre-moderns. Ancient and medieval people projected their spiritual life, their ideas about good and evil, their fears and aspirations, their very conception of 'spirit', onto forces outside themselves and did not understand, as we do, says Goitein, that all their ideas and beliefs originate in human consciousness. For example, when Abraham had decided to migrate to Canaan, he understood his decision as a divine call to 'go to the land that I shall show you'. Moderns, however, look to such realms of knowledge as Psychology (particularly Psychoanalysis), and Rationalist Philosophy to understand what transpires in the life of spirit.

Nevertheless, Goitein vehemently rejects all attempts to re-write the Bible. God is at the center of Jewish self-understanding: God is 'the foundation stone' of the Bible; without God one cannot understand the Bible's cosmology, its morality, its national aspirations and self-image, and its understanding of the personal-religious dimensions of life. Thus the human being is depicted in the Bible as seeking help from God, "my Rock and my Salvation", for God is with the individual in joy and suffering. He is thus, first, the source of individual salvation. Second, He is the God of the nation. Third, He is creator of the world; and fourth, he is the source of Israel's moral law.[6]

And so Jewish education is first and foremost based on the Bible, of which God is the central character. But how can that be if God is the object of human projections? Goitein's reply: By understanding God as the "Spirit of Israel". The spirit of God is thus a human spirit; hence one may declare that "God and Israel are one". Israel cannot conceive of its spirit without study of the Bible in which it comes to recognize that God is that on which this spirit rests.

With regard to the question of whether there is such a spiritual Being in actuality, we should expect Goitein to take an open-and-shut position: after all, has he not explained why modern people cannot acquiesce to a view that depicts God as independent of human consciousness, as *not* arising in human consciousness, but as a living God who speaks to humans and enters into a covenantal relationship with them?

Yet, perhaps surprisingly, he describes himself as agnostic, one who admits that *possibly* there is such a supreme Being. He adamantly decries the Hebraic atheism that he finds in resurgent Palestine and Israel, which he dismisses as a stance designed to 'short-circuit culture'. Is this unexpected proximity to religion a feature of his theology or is it a pedagogical translation? Is the writer saying that since children are unlikely to move towards a 'truer' conception of God without going through an anthropomorphic stage of development first, one may encourage such children by 'agreeing' with them, for a time? Or is he making a 'truth claim' that maybe there is a God and that, therefore, one dare not give non-belief a monopoly on self-evident truth?

Let us return from the world of conjecture to what Goitein actually says. Clearly, he insists on placing the Bible, with its God, at the center of Jewish curriculum. However is it the God of Jewish tradition? The fact that this question arises testifies that there has been a deep and fundamental translation, not only on a pedagogical level, but also on the plane of principle and verifiable truth claims. Is what Goitein doing a rejection of the religious tradition or a 'translation'?

Without doubt, a price has been paid for moving God into the realm of human spirit; whether for good or ill, something is 'lost in translation'. We shall briefly mention three significant items that thinkers who 'depersonalize' God and view His 'presence' as completely within the world of our perception and inquiry, seem to have lost in translation.

But before that, a qualifying thought. It could be argued that all these are abstract distinctions that need make no difference in actual life. Is it so important, for teachers and pupils alike, whether they think that the Bible is the testimony to the religious genius of the Jewish people, or whether God is believed to be an unequivocal actor in history and existence, who speaks to His people and commands them even when their 'spirit' is stubborn and rebellious? Is God a manifestation of Israel's spirit or its Judge? Does "the Giver of the Torah" speak from within or from without the "Tent of Meeting"?

But is it True?

The theologically-minded teacher – and pupil, like our two young people in the Negev and Haifa – will insist that the issue is important: they want to know what is true and what is false, and their teachers are likely to agree that distinctions must be made between 'translations based on truth claims' and pedagogical translations. We may state the position of these students by addressing the three issues – reverence and plausibility, transcendence, and responsibility – that get 'lost in translation':

1 – How can one stand in reverence before one's own spirit which, at times – as in the case of King Saul – experiences itself as bereft of "the spirit"? How can one worship the work of one's hands if we know that it is our own handiwork?

This is an issue raised by the midrash that depicts Abraham destroying the idols in his father's idol shop.[7] This midrash is so well known and so central in the classical narrative of Judaism, that many pupils and adults think that the story appears in the Bible itself. Here is the story:

The midrash relates that Abraham was asked by his father, Terach, to 'mind the shop' while he went out. Once left alone, Abraham proceeded to hack all the idols to smithereens. Upon his father's return, the latter furiously demanded an explanation. Abraham told him that the chief idol had grown angry at the others and, in a fit of rage, had demolished all the other idols. Terach quite reasonably did not accept this explanation. How could wooden idols *do anything*? Abraham pointed out that in this statement, Terach was expressing the futility of worshipping idols that have eyes but cannot see, and ears but cannot hear. Our midrashic teacher posits a critique of 'God as human spirit'. The point of the midrash is that it is ridiculous to bow down to an idol, that is, any handicraft of human artisans, to worship it as though it were not simply – handicraft! Who can, in all honesty, worship human ideas or artifacts – or ideals? How can the Israelites say so facilely of a golden calf, "This is your God, O Israel"? Who was there and did not see that this 'god' was made by men?

2 – A second cost of translation, our Haifa pupil has discovered, lies behind his research and raises the precise question that he asked his Bible teacher. It invites the distinction between the humane society and the Kingdom of God, between the good and the holy, between a pat on the back by the dedicated community worker and "the hand of God" upon Ezekiel. The distinction is that between the welfare state of *Tikkun Olam* on the one hand, and *Veyamlich Malkhutai* (Thy kingdom come) on the other.

Existentially, this distinction is not distant from the first one in which we saw Terach made a fool of, but it states the matter more philosophically. As in the first category, we have here a denial that any human handiwork – of exalted concepts such as sovereignty, or ideology – may be placed above humanity, even if they are unquestionably laudable.

The price paid for thorough-going translation, then, is the loss of transcendence. If all comes from the human spirit, who is the judge of that spirit which knows itself as flawed? If humanism is all there is in a moral stance and sensibility, what is to be done with failure and 'backsliding'? If "may Thy kingdom come (*vayamlich malkhutai*)" is a prayer for a welfare state that deals decently with its poor and that does good deeds and encourages its citizens to realize their potential, why pray for it? Isn't it enough to work for it? Is such a prayer, directed at the human spirit not an admission that the spirit that judges is no less fragile than the spirit that is judged?!

Of course, the prayer, *vayamlich malkhutai* while pointing in certain directions that we can experience as imbued with holiness, does not inform us what that 'kingdom' will look like, although only in reference to it people cry in longing and hope. The kingdom of God has the power to surprise and to confound our expectations. Without transcendence the capacity to "trust in God" is lost. Without transcendence, only the sentimental will cry at Yom Kippur's late afternoon plea: "At the hour of closing the gate (of atonement) open the gate for us." (What gate? What is meant by opening it? How is it not open until this very last moment?) How is it that this prayer sounds so metaphorical and poetic and whimsical, yet at certain times seems to be the rock upon which all reality rests? If the spirit of Jonah (i.e. the human being) is identical to the spirit of God, Jonah would have been spared the dilemma of choosing between God's will to save Nineveh and the national impulse to prophesy against Nineveh, the enemy of Israel, and to pray for its destruction.

3 – The third issue relates to responsibility. Is it our experience that we make significance and obligation, or that they are thrust upon us? That we are well-served by idols or that they are simply carved wood? Do we live by 'our values' or do we belong to them, even while they are, in some sense, chosen by us?

In the idols of Terach, then, and in the distinction between the welfare state and "Thy kingdom", and in the distinction that may be experienced between the intrinsically holy and the worthy, we come across the world of translation: from Theology to Psychology, Anthropology (where many find the sources of Theology), Philosophy, and Sociology. And then, having been in the realm of the objectively knowable, we discover an additional dimension: the experience of the holy that can change our perspectives. As the German Jewish philosopher, Franz Rosenzweig, expresses these problems of translation,

> Just as a student of William James knows how to put every 'religious experience' into the correct cubbyhole of the psychology of religion, and a Freudian student can analyze the experience into its elements of the old yet ever new story, so a student of Wellhausen will trace every commandment back to its human, folkloristic origin, and a student of Max Weber derive it from the special structure of a people.

Psychological analysts find the solution to all enigmas in self-delusion, and historical sociology finds it in mass delusion. The Law is not understood as a commandment addressed by God but as a soliloquy of the people. We know it differently, not always and not in all things, but again and again. For we know it only when – we *do*. What do we know when we do? Certainly not that all these historical and sociological explanations are false. But in the light of the doing, of the right doing in which we experience the reality of the Law, the explanations are of superficial and subsidiary importance. And in the doing, there is even less room for the converse wisdom...that these historical and sociological explanations may be true and that the Law is important because it alone guarantees the unity of the people in space and through time.[8]

One may wonder what Goitein would later teach his Bible students. Perhaps he believed that his description of reality would make his pupils 'insiders', that it was a translation that made the continuation of the tradition possible and plausible to young Jews sitting in the Israeli classroom. In such a case, perhaps he, who called Nehemiah Nobel "rabbi", thought that, though his translation came to less than what he personally believed, it might represent what is required to keep the "spirit of Israel" alive among the children of a secular age, in Israel as well as in the Diaspora. It is they who will, for better or for worse, be entrusted with the future of the Jewish people. So it might have seemed sensible to have recourse to whatever methods made the text and its tradition valuable, plausible and believable, and translation legitimate as a pedagogic enterprise. What, after all, is wrong with a Jewish education through which children are moved by the wars of Saul and David, in which they observe mitzvot, even if they do so as Jewish folkways?

Channels to Transcendence

Yet how can teachers who believe, with Goitein, that the spirit originates with humans, consider the possibility of "the living God"? How can room be made for the 'perhaps' of Goitein's agnostic approach?

Educators and thinkers who believe this to be a non-issue generally identify the values to which we wish to educate in the fabric and the content of (Jewish) culture itself. Thus, one who speaks the language of the Jews, is attached to their land, turns often and competently to Judaism's bookcase, is concerned for Jewish continuity and lives in fellowship with fellow Jews, especially on Sabbaths, feasts and fasts, has received a good Jewish education. *Yet all this, I suggest, is true only if one posits that the artifacts of Jewish culture are themselves the values towards which we educate.* Hence, if we have achieved this aim, our education has succeeded.

I suggest that this is a dubious position because culture itself is not primarily a system of binding values. One cannot in good conscience demand of anyone that he or she do what previous generations did, simply because they did it. To make culture itself the object of obligation and a demanding identity is problematic, even unfair, for it maps out one's future as synonymous with one's past. Why not rebel against such a deterministic conception? This, I think, is the theological ground for the belief that what is truly binding must incorporate the commandment of God.

The above might seem to suggest that socialization and acculturation into the life of the community and its heritage is worthless or even unacceptable. But in fact we know that we do see being drawn into the life of the community, discovering its treasures and observing its laws, as not only worthy but the focal activity of Judaism, and that its crown is learning Torah.

So we are in a paradoxical situation. If what we mean by success in education is to teach a cultural language of belonging, participating, doing and feeling, how can we maintain that 'culture' by itself is not normative while we build our educational institutions precisely on the social and existential centrality of 'culture'?

I suggest the following way of looking at this. The historical community of Israel has believed, for more than two thousand years, that there are channels of culture composed of laws and memories, institutions and halakhot, that came to be experienced as *mitzvot* and *emunah* (faith), and that education is the devout 'learning' of Torah. This conception is based on the distinction made by Rosenzweig between the Torah as law, as an 'objective code' of Judaism which is studied and observed because it is 'mine', and that which 'happens' to me when I experience 'the law' as now commanded to me. Stating this differently, it is not the patterns of culture that are 'demanded' as such.

These patterns are the channels through which all that is commanded reaches us. For this accessibility to become possible, education is a *sine qua non*. In Jewish education, then, we teach 'the law' in anticipation of the commandment; we express ideas about God, mainly in stories, and we do what Jews do to serve God and to prepare young people to recognize and then await the opportunity and capacity to address Him.

Teaching how to open the channels and to keep them open through a knowledge of Judaism and an attachment to it for its ability to convey values, revelation and commandments to us, is what Jewish education may see as its purpose. And the reward: to hear the teaching of God address *us* and to be attentive. Which laws in this context will be experienced as commandments, depends on many factors. Not every artifact, not every law or every biblical story or Talmudic teaching will turn magically into the living word of God. But since each of them has the capacity to do so, children must learn very many, as many as possible, so that there be ever more opportunities and 'openings to the divine'.

Ironically, then, less translation may be a key to Jewish learning. When the child asks what the "hand of God" means, he is asking about the unique experience of the prophet. When a child suggests that "everyone knows" what happens when the spirit of God leaves a person, it may be better to agree than to translate.

In summation, then, in Jewish education, one tends to speak mainly of socialization into Judaism rather than cultivating religious sensibility. For education, as Leibowitz pointed out,[9] is education for *mitzvot*. It is the inauguration and indeed induction of the young person into the channels, and instructions on how they work. It is institutional. It features the sacrament of 'learning Torah'. But all this is for the experience of "How I loved Your Torah", for reciting the Song of the Sea with a thrill of God's hand upon us, for appreciating that which flows through the channels. It is not for what we have learned that we appreciate Jewish life ultimately, but for the voice that may be heard within it.

But is it? Is this voice really heard or is even prayer simply another cultural gesture? This must have pre-occupied the young cantor Goitein who described himself as "the stranger in your midst". It must also have pre-occupied Rosenzweig.

As will be more fully discussed in subsequent essays, the experience to which we are pointing of God as explaining and 'organizing' all spiritual reality, comes to us through the channels of our culture, though adherence to culture is not yet by itself a normative affair. Nevertheless, one may experience the life of spirit and of the Spirit that is above it, through the agency of particular language, memory, society, culture. The prophet reporting that the hand of God was upon him, heard that which he heard and did what he did through the medium of the prophetic tradition of his people; he spoke in their tongue, and his vocabulary and his images bespoke the specific epoch in which he spoke. Nevertheless, religious believers will believe him when he says that he felt the hand upon him and will try to understand what he experienced as he was being spoken to and touched.

Likewise the forlorn king of Israel who felt the spirit of God deserting him, may be believed by those who have learned to take the biblical story seriously. The fact is that there are youngsters, like the boy we met in the 'secular' Haifa classroom, who are agitated by it and who ask whether it is permitted to them to wonder whether God's spirit is 'with' *them*. Here again the culture of the ancient Jewish narrator serves as a pointer to norms and commandments. But the commandment is not in knowing the story, or even in liking it, but in seeing oneself in it, in the current of one's life, waiting to hear what it means.

1. The term applied to Zionist Jews born in Palestine-Israel.

2. I Samuel 16ff

3. Numbers 15:26

4. Shlomo Dov Goitein, *Hora'at HaTanakh: Ba'ayoteiha vDarkeiha (Teaching Bible: Problems and Paths)*, Tel Aviv: Yavne Publishing House, 1957, pp. 9-10

5. Ibid.

6. Ibid., pp. 280ff.

7. Genesis Rabbah 38, Tanna Debei Eliyahu

8. Franz Rosenzweig, *On Jewish Learning*, N. N. Glatzer (ed.), Schocken Books, 1955, pp. 121-122

9. Isaiah Leibowitz, 'Education for Mitzvot', in David Weinstein and Michael Yizhar (eds.) *Readings in Jewish Thought*, Vol. I, Chicago: College of Jewish Studies, 1964, pp. 56-60 (Hebrew)

III

Educating 'in God's Presence': Testimony and Theology[1]

In this essay, I shall attempt to examine the role of theology in a situation that was perceived by many as miraculous, namely, the unanticipated and largely unprecedented victory of Israel in the Six-Day War. Unlike the discussions in the previous essay in which I explored the relationship of modern individuals to God and religious faith, here I am dealing with collective and historical experiences, indeed, events in which Providence seems actually encountered, and not only by those of religious mind sets and theological orientations to life. Here persons do not much speak of identity or "deep experience" but of astounding happenings, of a meeting between the people of Israel and the Divine in the context of the land that the Bible calls "God's portion". These great happening are seen as forming and constituting a collective memory, forged by their meeting in storm and fire yet tempered by halakhic and moral discipline.

Our discussion here of the Six-Day War points to various options. These options are, to some extent, still with us and are even at times accentuated by current events and ideological shifts. Therefore the following discussion should be seen as typological, and not as a report on these current events.

Michael Rosenak

What do the events of June 1967 and their aftermath teach us about the uses of theology, and where are the limits of theological discourse in such situations? And prior to these questions: What is, in fact, 'a religious reaction' to a startling historical event like the Six-Day War, so heavily laden with relief, gratitude and joy at the unexpected salvation, yet bearing the imprint, too, of perplexity and bereavement? I shall begin by relating four of many comments and episodes that come to mind, snatches of speech that may suggest parameters for our discussion.

One kibbutz member, an educator and a learned farmer, (a complex type of Jewish person that was the pride and ideal of the religious kibbutz in its formative years) wrote in the monthly journal of his kibbutz movement:

> Who in Israel or in the world would have believed *that after a battle of 132 hours* Israel would have in its hands Jerusalem and the place of our sanctuary... all of Western Eretz Yisrael... all the Sinai Peninsula till the Suez Canal? It is all exactly written in the book of Joshua: 'And no man stood up to them of all their enemies... Nothing was lacking of all the good things which the Lord had spoken...'
>
> Master of the Universe: May this be an hour of mercy before You. Lest our spirits become arrogant and we say... 'Our strength and the might of our hands have wrought this great deed'. But let us know... that we have merited to live in an epoch in which God has returned to His people... And our very eyes have seen this![2]

A man from another religious kibbutz writes home from the front:

> In the air hung a sense of great and holy hours. When I asked a fellow-soldier, a member of Kibbutz Sha'ar Ha'amakim, at the Rockefeller Museum, before the conquest of the Temple Mount, 'what have you got to say?' he answered me with a verse from the Bible. 'I was glad when they said unto me, let us go to the house of the Lord. Our feet were standing in thy gates Jerusalem, Jerusalem, that is built as a city that is tied together'. The fellow smiled as he cited this verse. Maybe because it isn't fitting for a member of Hashomer Hatzair to speak thus. But I saw his eyes and I knew that that was what he felt.[3]

A professor of Jewish Thought who lived in North America, remarked on the months of waiting and trepidation before the war:

> On [a certain] public occasion, in March 1967, I asked the following question: Would we (like Job) be able to say that the question of Auschwitz will be answered in any sense whatever in case the eclipse of God were ended and He appeared to us? An impossible and intolerable question.
>
> Less than three months later, this purely hypothetical question had become actual, when at Jerusalem the threat of total annihilation gave way to sudden salvation, atheists spoke of miracles and hardboiled Western reporters resorted to Biblical images.

> The question *is* impossible and intolerable. Even Job's question is not answered by God's presence, and to him children are restored. The children of Auschwitz will not be restored and the question of Auschwitz will not be answered by a saving divine presence.[4]

And another thinker-soldier:

> Peace in the world will not be built on the foundations of readiness to compromise... I maintain that if there be concessions on Eretz Yisrael, there will also be concessions on peace in the world and the redemption of the world.[5]

Euphoria and Faith

Which of these qualify (or qualify more) as religious responses? Is a religious response only (or mainly) one of a religious person, articulating religious perceptions, or is it (also) a 'religiously heavy' statement or outburst, also when made by a 'secularist'? What is the status of a philosophical exploration, made in the wake of an historical happening? And what about an ideological pronouncement about the consequences of an event and its normative significance, made from a religious perspective? In examining and clarifying these questions, I shall have recourse to two categories of response: testimony – spontaneous and unmediated; and theology – reflective, sometimes comprehensive, often ideological.

A search for the first type of response, of testimony, takes us back to Independence Day 1967.

From Independence Day – 1967

Each of us Jews knows how thoroughly ordinary he is: yet, taken together, we seem caught up in things great and inexplicable. It is almost as if we were not acting but being acted through... The number of Jews in the world is smaller than a small statistical error in the Chinese census. Yet... big things seem to happen around us and to us.[6]

In numerous articles, letters and conversations, Israeli and Diaspora Jews testified to acting and 'being acted through' in a drama that placed them, however temporarily, in a dimension of existence they had never known. This drama and dimension had something 'religious' about it, if only because routine secular assumptions appeared suddenly inadequate, even trivial, and, for a while at least, religious experiences – and religious people – seemed more serious, as though they knew more about the mysterious Actor and His unfolding plot.

The drama may be said to have begun on Independence Day, 1967. It was then, on the evening of 14 May, that the news reached Israel of Egyptian forces on the move into the Sinai. That day, however, despite worry, the country was celebrating. The highlight of the holiday, as was usual in those years, was a military parade, held at that year's Independence Day celebrations in Jerusalem. The parade was a small one, conscientiously held to the dimensions of men and equipment mandated by the demilitarized status of Jerusalem, a city distrustfully shared by Israel and Jordan. Thus the celebration highlighted the pain associated with Jerusalem, divided by a wall and largely inaccessible. On that same evening, at the annual Independence Day Song Festival, Jerusalem was again brought into consciousness when a young singer, Shuli Natan, performed Naomi Shemer's new song, *Yerushalayim shel Zahav* (Jerusalem of Gold), a sentimental ballad of love and longing about the "city that dwells abandoned and at whose heart stands a Wall". None of the listeners suspected that, within a few short weeks, the song would become a kind of anthem, and that a new stanza would be added: "We have returned... the Shofar is sounded on the Temple Mount".

In retrospect, perhaps the most startling episode of testimony of that day took place in a Jerusalem yeshiva,[7] *Mercaz Harav Kook*, established by the first Chief Rabbi of modern *Eretz Israel* and then led by his son, Rabbi Zvi Yehudah Kook. Of the 'higher Yeshivot', this yeshiva was perhaps the only one radically Zionist in orientation, for here a fervent nationalist ideology was fostered and Independence Day was celebrated with a uniquely pious and festive solemnity. In his address at the Independence Day celebration, Rabbi Zvi Yehudah agitatedly confided to his students that, while crowds had rushed into the streets to dance on the day of Partition in 1947, he had sat and mourned at what he viewed as the grim fulfillment of the prophecy of Joel (4:2): 'And My Land they have divided'. As *Davar* reporter, Danny Rubenstein, was later to describe it:

His veteran students, who had learned Torah from him for years and were used to taking part in the traditional Independence Day celebration at the *Yeshiva*, say that for nineteen years Rav Zvi Yehudah had not told of his weeping... on the day of partition. And now, in May 1967, he continued... in a loud shout of anguish: Where is our Schechem (Nablus)? Where is our Jericho? Where is our (river) Jordan?

Two weeks later, the students of the Yeshiva were already mobilized... They [shortly thereafter] passed through Schechem and Jericho bearing with them an overpowering experience – perhaps prophecy, perhaps 'a heavenly voice' that had come from the mouth of their rabbi.[8]

In the days and weeks following, Israel mobilized, negotiated, prepared. U Thant evacuated United Nations troops from Sinai and Gaza with an alacrity that may well have surprised even Nasser. The former ally, de Gaulle, turned indifferent, even hostile. The Western world urged patience and at the UN compromises and arrangements were proposed that were based on the assumption (or perhaps, hope) of Israel's absolute vulnerability. In Israel, public parks were quietly, indeed secretly, prepared as consecrated ground for the eventuality of mass burials. The Holocaust, in growing public consciousness since the Eichmann trial in 1961, arose in every mind as a memory and renewed possibility. Muki Tzur, reminiscing in a book of 'Soldiers' Talk', described it:

> We tend to forget those days before the war... but those were the days in which we came very close to that Jewish destiny from which we fled... Suddenly everybody began talking of Munich, of the Holocaust, of the Jewish people that had been abandoned to its fate.[9]

On 3 June, the Sabbath before the outbreak of the war, I attended the synagogue of *Bet Hillel*, of the Hebrew University. Most of the seats were empty, the members mobilized. The section of the Torah read that day included the *Tochecha*, the dreaded punishments to be meted out to Israel for betraying the Covenant. The congregation sat through these half-whispered Torah passages depressed, almost in a daze.

At 10 o'clock on the morning of 5 June, Michael Elkins of the BBC reported from Jerusalem that the Egyptian air force had been destroyed and that Israel had won the war. Both CBS and the BBC, not attuned to the miraculous, held up the story for several hours. [10] Perhaps they lost a scoop; perhaps Hussein lost the information that might have saved him Jerusalem and the West Bank. He could, of course, learn nothing from the Israeli media, which reported only vaguely on sporadic bombardments. By evening, while Jerusalem was being shelled, the news spread through the country: 'We're winning'. The speed and scope of the victory created an atmosphere and a feeling in the public that was, as Eliezer Schweid well described it, "on the threshhold" of a religious sentiment.[11] Unlike the War of Independence of 1948, notes Schweid, this campaign was unexpectedly short and the achievements were greater than the expectations. Others commented that the insistence of Jordan's King Hussein to participate in the war – thus 'assuring' the liberation of Jerusalem – could be understood only in the biblical idiom: evidently, God had 'hardened his heart'.

All this and Jerusalem too!

The return of the Jewish people, through its army, to the heartland of *Eretz Israel* and to Old Jerusalem was experienced as startling by many who had thought that it, and its most 'traditional' landmark, the *Kotel Ha-Ma'aravi* (Western Wall), meant nothing to them. In the words of one soldier:

> When we [in our unit] were riding to Jerusalem, some people were standing next to [Kibbutz] Huldah and shouting: 'The *Kotel* ...the *Kotel*, the *Kotel!!!*' These words, nothing else... For all of us in the bus that was enough. I have no religious inclinations, no one can suspect me of that. But that was something that touched all of us, that meant more than anything else.[12]

In the days of the battle for Jerusalem and its conquest, the focus of Zionism seemed to move, from the coast and the fabled Jezreel Valley to the mountains of Judea; from Tel Aviv, the 'all-Jewish city', to Jerusalem, the 'sanctuary of the King', and its only remaining concrete symbol, the Western Wall [the *Kotel*]. Andre Neher[13] has remarked on the dialectic of paratroopers, who had never given a thought to the *Kotel*, passing through the Meah Shearim quarter (an ultra-religious neighborhood in Jerusalem) on their way to its conquest. In Meah Shearim, despite the *Kotel's* inaccessibility, it had remained a living presence, but the people there had neither the actual aspiration nor the physical strength or training to fight for it. This strength only the paratroopers had; they were the ones who made the *Kotel* again accessible to the faithful, and when they reached the Wall they were startled to find themselves crying, perhaps with tears long stored up in the ultra-Orthodox sections of Jerusalem. The bond between *haredim* (ultra-Orthodx) and 'freethinking' warriors, expressed even in physical embraces, was not destined to outlive those short weeks. But when it appeared, it appeared as exhilarating, miraculous, messianic.

At the same time, there is testimony that the days of fighting brought a new generation, grown to adulthood since the War of Independence, into confrontation with the paradoxes that mark even a 'miraculously successful' war. Together with the joy of the *kibbutznik* from Sha'ar Ha'amakim, 'glad to go to the house of the Lord', there was death – and killing. A soldier relates:

> During the battle we killed an Egyptian officer.... among his papers, I see a picture of two little children, smiling at the seashore, and a letter in a feminine handwriting ... I thought: What is the feeling of a family in the kibbutz when a son is killed? And here I killed the father of two children... Of course, these were soldiers who were fighting us... But nevertheless.[14]

The paradox and the tension are well stated in one Orthodox soldier's description of a shattering existential moment:

> A fellow with a transistor next to his ear shouts: 'Quiet! Quiet! Let's hear the news'. Suddenly his eyes brighten. *'Chevre! Chevre!* [Hey, guys!] The Old City of Jerusalem is in our hands.' I stand in a daze; it is hard for me to believe the news ... Suddenly, shouts: 'Airplanes!' ... from the direction of the setting sun, a Mig appears... A cloud of smoke arises in front of us. I lie flat, cover my head with my helmet, and a flashing thought passes through my mind: Now? [To die] now? Jerusalem! No! No![15]

But soldiers reported on moral dilemmas and confrontations as well as existential paradoxes. One soldier relates: "The moment I was in Gaza, and I saw that we were winning the war and were about to become an army of conquest, I sat my men down and told one of them... to read the story of Achan [who took booty from Jericho] in the Book of Joshua. If anything influenced my men on how to act as a conquering army, it was this chapter."[16] Soldiers perceived that religion, despised by many of them and alien to most, might, in its symbols and gestures, hold a key to the paradoxes and provide a language for moral deliberation, provide a cultural context even for the pain of bereavement. Rena Barzilai of Kibbutz Ha'Ogen[17] writes on the evening the war ended:

> Six hundred and seventy nine emissaries
> O Master of the Universe, to You,

To the kingdom of the King of all kings
To your holy land we dispatched....
Wounded, ragged they will appear before You
To intercede for us before the throne of glory. [18]

On the morning of Shavuot (Pentecost), 14 June, the public at large was given access to the Western Wall and 200,000 came to it, or rather, stormed it on that day. Beginning at two and three o'clock in the morning, Jews thronged the road leading to the *Kolel*, to be there on time for *Shacharit* (morning) prayers, which began simultaneously in scores of *minyanim*[19] at 4 a.m. Arab citizens kept indoors out of sight. The encounter with that problem, with that people, lay in the future and few Jews thought of them or were distracted by them that morning. It was experienced as a rare moment. Those who met at the Wall hailed one another and exchanged tearful wishes of *mazal tov* ('congratulations'). From Independence Day until Shavuot, it seemed, the exile had finally ended. How could there be less than undreamed-of joy?

But that, even in those days, was not the whole story. During that very week, religious and non-religious Jews paid many visits to newly-bereaved families. Religious Zionists tended to exchange the traditional formulation of comfort, "May you be comforted among the mourners of Zion and Jerusalem" with a new one: "May you be consoled in the consolation of Zion". Apparently, those who did so felt, as Harold Fisch wrote,[20] that the mourning of Zion was at an end. Whether that was the case – and, if so, what it meant – was to become the subject of long and heart-searching discussions.

Since Shavuot 1967: Theologies of Response

Many 'secular' as well as 'religious' Jews experienced *something* during the Six-Day War and testified to it. Yet it must be clear that while "testimony" arises out of genuine feeling, it is to be distinguished from theology of response. The former is 'an experience', perhaps even one never to be forgotten, but theology is an ongoing endeavor to understand the foundation stones of religious faith and to buttress conviction by 'thinking through' not only what happened but, also, what it may mean. Hence, only those who have a stake in – and ongoing concern with – religious meaning feel that they must theologize. Testimony can rest on feeling alone; systematic religious response requires an on-going, growing and integrating conception.

The theological or narrative-religious responses to the Six-Day War were, after the initial euphoria, extremely varied. They flowed, to a large extent, from what Bellah has termed "habits of the heart"[21] and from concern with three fundamental, inter-locked issues:

(a) How may one view the relationship between history and Torah? What is the spiritual significance of the present vis-à-vis the (sacred) past and the anticipated (messianic) future?

(b) How shall one, committed to the sacred past and the messianic future, relate to Zionism – a Jewish movement

113

in history, committed and directed categorically to the significance of the present?

(c) What are some other options? Six theological positions.

(a) History and Torah

What the relationship should be between historical events and the actual 'life of Judaism' is very problematic in the Jewish tradition; in modern Jewry, emphatically so. Why is this?

Evidently, the tradition 'takes history very seriously'; it sees the hand of God in the Exodus, in the conquest of Canaan and even in the destruction of the Temple. Yet Israel is repeatedly warned not to be deceived by false prophets who promise salvation without authorization, and not to be shattered by historical tribulations; the essential thing is to be steadfast with God, which means to obey His commandments. We are told to see God's great hand in history, but in epochs of Divine eclipse, not to take this history as conclusive – and to wait patiently for the Messiah. Thus, the *hope* of Judaism is the advent of the Messianic era, but the actual *life* of Judaism is the Torah and its commandments. Because history is serious – but subservient to Torah – theology cannot be divorced from history; but it may with impunity be severed from particular historical realities that have been 'neutralized', as it were. Shalom Rosenberg has pointed out that the Sages gave Hannukah[22] halakhic permanence as the Independence Celebration of the Macabbean state, even though that state had already been destroyed.[23] In a similar vein, the iconoclastic theologian, Isaiah Leibowitz, who insisted that "This bloody mess which is called History only reflects the wickedness and idiocy of man" and who consistently urged the immediate and unilateral relinquishing of 'the territories', admitted after the war that:

> One thing will remain with us from all this. The twenty-eighth of *Iyar* [in the Hebrew calendar]. The day on which we took Jerusalem. I'm not sure that we will keep the city, but the [commemorative] day will remain.[24]

Yet, when the Messiah does come, obviously history, theology and reality can no longer be kept apart. And what if the tremendous series of events of 1967, coming after the beginning of Return and in the wake of the Holocaust, is indeed the redemption? In that case, is 'returning to the routine of Jewish life' by, say, fasting on the seventeenth of Tammuz (to mark the ancient Babylonian breach of the walls of Jerusalem) not ingratitude and rebellion where, in other times, it would have been perceived as pristine loyalty to Torah and Halakhah?[25]

In the contemporary era, the problem of 'History-and-Torah' is confounded by the historical crisis of Judaism, characterized by the widespread abandonment of the age-old 'actual life of Judaism' – that is, of the regimen of the *mitzvot*.[26] Zionism, as anti-Zionist traditionalists have pointed out as emphatically as the Zionists themselves, is built on the premise that Jews need not be observant in order to be loyal Jews. They must simply return to their own land and take their place on the stage of history. Pious traditionalists have called this False Messianism; most Zionists have (perhaps romantically) termed it realism. But what should the realists do when they seem to be in the presence of miracles? How should the pietists react when the secularists seem to be 'returning to Judaism' because history appears to have vindicated Jewish tradition for them? Should the stubborn upholders of the tradition call this authentic redemption – or false prophecy?

Furthermore, in the age of crisis, can even religious Zionist Jews state categorically what 'the life of the commandments' is – and that it demands of everyone that it be lived as in the past? Is not the 'secular' Jew instructing his men in the biblical story of Achan – so that they will not loot – in fact teaching them Torah? Is the *kibbutznik* engaged in the conquest of Jerusalem and declaring his gladness at ascending 'to the house of the Lord' perhaps *praying* even while occupied with the *mitzvah* of Jewish self-defense? Conversely, in the present historical situation, do we know that the 'obvious' halakhic content of Judaism is, in toto, still commanded? Now that 'the Old City of Jerusalem is in our hands', are we to rebuild the Temple and offer sacrifices – and tear down the Mosque of Omar? And assuming for sundry reasons, that it does not or cannot mean that, how about sacrificing the Passover lamb which can be offered without rebuilding the Temple? Why does no one do that?[27] Are, then, the prayers of 'the religious' for the restoration of the Temple service insincere? Or are they serious only for 'when the Messiah comes'? Or shall we now, by force of will, welcome the opportunity to 'restore our days as of old', and plan actively for whatever the Messianic times, about to commence, will demand of us?

(b) Between Sacred Past and Messianic Future

Nahum Arieli has posited[28] that what distinguishes secular Zionism from traditionalism is that the latter strives to live its Judaism within the sacred past, looking towards an anticipated redeemed future. In this scheme of things, the present is devoid of significance. One lives, as it were, alongside of it, trying to ignore it, gladly leaving its functioning to the gentiles, building bridges from past to future which span and distractedly look down on it. On the other hand, the secular Zionist rebels against the past and seeks collective self-realization in the present. The future, which is the immediate continuation of the present, depends on what we do now.

Arieli saw in classic religious Zionism a third option – that of remaining loyal to the sacred past and working to channel its contents into a relevant and responsible present. This third way is opposed equally by the ultra-Orthodox and by consistent secularists. The greatest test of religious Zionism comes when the Messiah, who is 'believed in' – if only because the anticipation of his coming is part of the sacred past – may be plausibly expected *in the present*. The 'real' traditionalists who 'know' that he cannot possibly come on the wings of heretical Zionism, for whom 'the Jewish state' is simply another 'present-ness' to be negotiated and overcome, do not have this problem. Neither are those secularists who have no loyalty to the

Messianic faith troubled. The "crisis of Messianism", in Werblowsky's[29] pithy phrase, is a religious-Zionist one. Because of their commitment to the present, religious Zionists are embarrassed by traditional Messianism. Yet, because of their commitment to the past, they cannot abandon the hope and expectation.

The question of the relationship to past, present and future may, of course be linked to Zionism in a simple and straightforward manner: those who are Zionists have 'sold out' to the present; 'true' Jews, who maintain their indifference and hostility to the present, cannot be Zionists. This is the *Haredi* (ultra-Orthodox) position.

In fact, this is an oversimplification, for one can be a Zionist and remain loyal to tradition in one of two ways. First, one may be a purely 'political Zionist' who will have no truck with new normative 'Jewish culture' where such culture contravenes or supersedes the tradition. Such political Zionism is viewed by its religious adherents as 'merely' a solution to 'the problem of the Jews' who wish neither to be undermined by the culture of the gentiles nor to be slaughtered by them. It is simply another strategy for dealing with the present, providing a better plane on which to survive for the life of Torah and to wait for the Messiah.

A second option is to look upon Zionism as a consummation of traditional Judaism, as "the beginning of our Redemption". In this view, Zionism not only does not require the abrogation of the traditional Torah, but is providentially charged to restore errant Jews to the domain of the Torah – through the historical dynamic it initiates.

Thus, in the case of 'dry' political Zionism, nothing that happens has religious meaning for its religious partisan; God continues to be 'absent', outside the realm of immediate Torah practice. Conversely, for theological Messianic Zionists, everything means something and the urge to interpret and 'understand' becomes particularly great in 'great moments'. Secular-minded Zionists are likely to fear the Messianic ones as irresponsible and to pity the Orthodox political ones for their halakhic 'fixations'. And between two types of religious Zionists, especially if they are consistent, we may expect to find lively polemics.

(c) Some Other Options: Six Theological Positions

In all religious responses to the Six-Day War, we shall find positions and 'understandings', not only on the religious significance of history, but on the theological weight to be placed on the present. Likewise, we may expect discrete views of Zionism, as either understanding and responding to the theological significance of the historical hour, or as false Messianism. In any case, we may expect religious discourse to assume and emphasize some connections between the historical hope of Judaism – its Messianic dimension – and the existential life of Judaism – in the Torah and its commandments.

Our six positions may be viewed as follows:

(a) Active Messianism;
(b) The Celebration of Salvation as Historical Vindication;
(c) Gratitude for God's Miracles;

    (d) Zionist Moral *Halakhism*;

    (e) Zionist Negation of Religious Historical Significance; and

    (f) Anti-Zionist Negation of Alleged Present Historical Significance.

(a) Active Messianism

The young men who participated in the Independence Day celebration at the Mercaz Harav Yeshiva felt strongly, during the war and after it, that they were living in Messianic times, that the anticipated future was – now. They and their teachers had carefully studied rabbinic texts which explained that the actual Messianic redemption is characterized by developments that they themselves had been witnessing: the Ingathering of the Exiles, political sovereignty, making the desert bloom and the conquest of the Land. The Six-Day War was thus a radical movement forward towards total redemption. In the words of Rabbi O. Hadya, the events of the war and the victory were "an astounding divine miracle... the end of days has already come... now through conquest *Eretz Israel* has been redeemed from oppression, from the *sitra achra* [Satan's camp]. It has entered the realm of sanctity."[30] To this, of course, there is an halakhic corollary: 'If, God forbid, we should return even a tiny strip of land we would thereby give control to the evil forces, to the *sitra achra*'.[31]

God, therefore, is acting to redeem us *now*, and if we fail to understand this and thus act to sabotage the redemption, we shall only prolong the painful 'birth pangs of the Messiah'. Thus, Ephraim Yair, in an article written shortly after the war, declares that God has had to give us (back) portions of our land three times in the storm of war (in the War of Independence, the Sinai Campaign and the Six-Day War) because "we keep on returning them". If we return the land again, we shall not be promoting peace thereby but forcing upon God another move to restore our land to us, i.e., by way of another war. The paradoxical result is that only an uncompromising position will bring peace to the area and the world.[32]

A similarly deterministic position, albeit milder in tone, sees a kind of biblical redemption in the events of our time: the Holocaust and the return to Israel are analogous to the slavery in Egypt and the Exodus. For example, Spero applies Buber's concept of 'the leading God' who took Israel out of Egypt, to the circumstances of those days:

> When today, in fact, a Jewish population [then] of three million inhabit the land in its biblical boundaries including Jerusalem and constitute the sovereign state of Israel, then the message of the events comes into... sharper focus. The God of Israel is *leading* His people back to the land... The invitation has turned into a summons.[33]

The *mitzvah* is clear: to go up to the land and settle it; to follow the leading God.

The disciples of Rabbi Zvi Yehudah Kook also translated the present – allegedly redemptive – events into *halakhic* categories. They have frequently cited Nachmanides' ruling that "we are commanded to enter the land, to conquer its cities and to settle our tribes there" as well as the prohibition he formulates: not to return any part of it to gentiles and not to leave it lying waste. Porat deduces from this even the *mitzvah* of working the land, for "he who leaves his land a wasteland... and uncultivated, transgresses against a negative commandment".[34] Thus, the Zionist ethos of *kibbush hashemama* (conquest of the wasteland) is given halakhic sanction within the theology of a present 'age of Redemption'. The 'future-that-is-now' is firmly anchored in the norms of the sacred past.

(b) Salvation as Historical Vindication

Unlike the first position, that was represented by a publicly visible ideological group, the *Gush Emunim* (Bloc of the Faithful) who have been the leading exponents of religious settlement on the West Bank, the second position represents an orientation, a religious mood. It is the mood of those who believe that the stirring events of the Six-Day War must be seen as religiously significant. They view the Zionist enterprise as not indifferent to the covenant between God and Israel, though they refuse to draw deterministically-redemptive conclusions from this. In this conception, a clear distinction should be drawn between God's *salvation* *(yeshuah)* and His *redemption (geulah),* between events like Purim[35] and events like the Exodus, though it is hoped that we will be worthy of seeing the present salvation as 'the beginning of our Redemption'. What characterizes this approach is, on the one hand, a 'realistic' view of history with its dangers, tragedies and complexities and, on the other hand, a belief that God is still with His people, Israel, and guards them. Israel is a singular people and is witness to *God in history*. Zionism, though a consequence of crisis and riddled with problems, testifies to the way Judaism can bear witness in the present; it sets a stage for God's expression of His sovereignty over men and nations.

The scholar-statesman, Yaakov Herzog, articulated this position in another way. Addressing representatives of religious *kibbutzim* in 1968, he related how, after the Six-Day War, he traveled to Rome to discuss the future of Jerusalem with church officials. Upon Herzog's return home, the Greek Patriarch Benedictus of Jerusalem summoned him to remind him that he, Benedictus, too had the status of a pope and that Israel should treat with him, a friend, when discussing Jerusalem with the Christian world. Herzog relates that, as the Patriarch was speaking, he recalled the antecedents of the Greek Patriarchate. It was established, Herzog notes, in the year 451, to solemnly declare that the city belonged to the Church, that it had been taken from the Jewish people in perpetuity. Thus, for Jews, the initiation of the line of Patriarchs was an historical hour of trauma and tragedy. He continues:

> And I thought to myself that if, at that time, a Jew had come into a synagogue in Rome, or Crete, or Alexandria, and said to another: "Have you heard? They want to seal the doom of Jerusalem, to cut us off forever from this city. They have appointed a 'Patriarch'," and the other had replied: "Despair not, my friends, because 1500 years hence a Jewish official of the Government of Israel will visit the descendant of the Patriarch now appointed and the ninety-fifth

descendant will say: The city is yours; it is united under Providence. You have found the road. All I ask is that you recognize my rights as well" ... those who heard such a statement would have thought the speaker a madman.[36]

What is the halakhah of this historical hour of salvation? It is to keep faith with God as He has kept faith with Israel in enabling the creation of the State of Israel, to use the opportunities accorded by the hour with moral intelligence and to hope that this may indeed be the beginning of redemption. Though one cannot know whether it is the harbinger of redemption, one can act with responsibility, dignity and a sense of religious wonder.[37]

(c) Gratitude for God's Miracles

The belief that God had 'shown His mighty hand', that the Six-Day War had a clearly miraculous dimension, appears to be close to the previous position which celebrates God's salvation. Yet in this orientation the emphasis is more likely to be pedagogic than theological: Jews should now 'see the light' and 'return'. The 'there were miracles' position tends to generate the wonder-of-dependence rather than the confidence-of-covenant. The miracle may thus be viewed as divine aid to survive the present for the sake of the still distant future rather than as an indication of the religious significance of the present. Consequently, very varied groups of people – from Habad Hasidim, scholarly and simple residents of Meah Shearim and secular Jews – have joined religious Zionists in expressing the conviction that 'we have witnessed miracles'. Likewise, Jews who previously did not generally blend religious and national sentiments, declared that 'we can depend only on God' (and not on 'seemingly friendly' nations).[38] An interesting listing of the miracles performed for Israel is given by Rabbi S. Y. Levin, editor of the renowned Talmudic Encyclopedia and respected sage. Among these miracles are mentioned the victory of Israel; the swiftness of the campaign which saved many casualties; the decision of Jordanian King Hussein to join the war which made the liberation of Jerusalem possible; the hesitancy of Prime Minister Eshkol before the war which had 'many positive results': the unity of the Jewish people in Israel and the Diaspora, and the awakening to eternal values. Especially critical was Israel's fighting alone, without the participation of other nations, thus becoming an instrument for the fulfillment of the biblical vision, "And the Lord alone shall be exalted on that day."[39]

A significant halakhic aspect of this approach is to be found in the decision of the Chief Rabbinate to establish the day of the conquest of Jerusalem as a holiday – Jerusalem Day – to be marked by the recitation of the entire *Hallel*,[40] replete with the traditional blessing. This was more than the Chief Rabbinate had permitted for Independence Day. With regard to the latter, the ambivalence of the rabbinical establishment vis-à-vis the secular Zionist state could not be overcome. As Chief Rabbi Unterman intimated:

> The victory in the Six-Day War – with all due respect and honor to our valiant soldiers... was miraculous

in every sense of the word... We cannot allow this miracle wrought by God to be unmarked by recitation of the full *Hallel* with the Blessing.

As for Independence Day, it is "also a great thing worthy of public celebration ... but this does not obligate the recitation of the full *Hallel* with the Blessing, or suspension of the Sefirah[41] restrictions, as in the case of Jerusalem Day, when we palpably saw a miracle occur."[42]

(d) Zionist Moral Halakhism

This approach may be briefly stated as follows: We have been placed in an historical situation which constitutes a test of our ability and willingness to be a people of the Torah, representing and articulating the moral sensitivity and the moral norms which are the soul of the halakhic tradition. Those who adhere to this position therefore hold that the present historical hour of divine deliverance now awaits human sanctification through an understanding of Torah which is morally adequate to the unprecedented challenges that face us – of return to the land and collective Jewish responsibility in our state. (Since both this return and the life of the state were made possible by Zionism, Zionism is a political movement of great spiritual weight, requiring serious theological attention and religious care.)

The position of Active Messianism is denounced in this approach for suggesting that holiness is inherent in the people of Israel regardless of Jewish actions, for intimating that the holiness of the land lies in some inherent ('magical') qualities, rather than in the Torah's charge that here Jews are to live a holy life as a people.

The Six-Day War gave Israel not only the exhilaration of God's salvation, but the responsibility *and the capacity* to seek compromise and peace. This view highlights that Judaism teaches that the real warrior is one who turns his enemy into a friend,[43] who is sensitive to the rights also of the other and who does not view Messianism as a narrow political conception, assuring territorial gains and military victories. Redemption must be left to God – He has entrusted to us the Torah, whose ways are the ways of pleasantness and peace. In the words of Aviezer Ravitsky, a prominent member of the religious peace movement:

> Peace, human dignity and justice – are these but 'western' values? Our conviction was, and remains, that these humanitarian values are also our own, and even fundamentally those of the Torah ...
>
> The conquest [in the Six-Day War] of East Jerusalem and of territories that once were part of Israel triggered a profound joy among the religious youth ... But in a short time, that joy slid into a sort of blind and intransigent passion that implicitly was isolated from other Jewish values... Of what did the prophets come to speak with the kings? Of 'Greater Israel'? Certainly not. They supported justice and righteousness.[44]

(e) Zionist Negation of Religious Historical Significance

In this view, it is posited that temporal events have no religious meaning: *only the Torah and its commandments constitute Judaism.* Indeed, our historical situation does make demands, but they are rational and moral; secular people can understand these requirements as well as religious ones.

This position, stated most consistently by Isaiah Leibowitz, juxtaposes the Halakhah and history. God *demands* adherence to the Torah but He *gives* nothing but religious human stature to those who accept the yoke of the Torah. Belief in salvational events is a delusion and, politically, it leads to reckless and foolish behavior. Zionism, an historical movement of Jews who were 'fed up with living among the gentiles', has nothing to do with salvation; indeed, the religious and secular Jews who make up this movement cannot possibly, without utterly corrupting the term, have a common conception of salvation. Thus, Leibowitz defines all Jewishly meaningful terms in a halakhic context:

> Never were holidays of remembrance or thanksgiving instituted in commemoration of victories and conquests. Even the Hasmoneans[45] – who are so often mentioned today in the current context – are cited in the sources and in the tradition solely for their *battle to preserve the Torah*... Furthermore, the whole concept of 'bravery' in Judaism is not confined to physical might. 'One should arise like the lion', the opening words of the *Shulchan Arukh*,[46] are directed not towards the soldier but towards one arising to worship God.[47]

Though this sounds like an *Agudist*[48] (anti-Zionist) position, it is here a radically political-Zionist one. Physical and military bravery on behalf of Israel is important, because

Israelis legitimately wish to have their own state. But this is not a religious wish or need; it is a human one, shared by pietists and atheists alike. What these different types of Jews disagree about is 'the life of *mitzvot*'; in this disagreement, which seemed at times to forebode civil war, the Six-Day War is irrelevant.

(f) Anti-Zionist Negation of Present Historical Significance

This position may be stated as follows: There is no positive meaning in the Six-Day War, and the very notion that there might be is ludicrous. Zionism is a heresy and the *Galut* (exile) continues, in *Eretz Israel* perhaps more than elsewhere, because of the pernicious Zionists. Zionism is the worst heresy imaginable; moreover, it is a cosmic catastrophe, impeding the redemption and strengthening satanic forces in the world. Not only is it not a legitimate response to the Holocaust, but it is, in fact, the very cause of it, for it spearheads a rebellion against God and impudently seeks to 'force the end'. The Six-Day War, as other seeming achievements or victories of Israel, are nothing but satanic lures, tempting the faithful (consisting predominantly of Satmar *Hasidim* and *Neturei Karta*)[49] and leading the State of Israel to well-deserved perdition. The truly faithful do well, therefore, not even to pray at the Western Wall, for it was conquered by the satanic Zionists.

This position has been most lucidly and radically expressed by Rabbi Joel Teitlebaum, leader of the Satmar *Hasidic* group.[50] While the extreme negative and demonic features of this theology are rejected by the more moderate

Agudat Yisrael, the latter agree that neither Israel nor the Six-Day War have positive religious meaning. Whereas the *Neturei Karta* sees these (the state and the war) with a hating negation, those to the left of them in the ultra-Orthodox community are characterized by indifference and varying degrees of contempt for the claims and enthusiasms of the Zionists.

* * *

Half a Century Later

Where does all this leave us with regard to Arieli's categories of history, messianism, and concrete claims of practical reality? In conclusion, let us try to gain a perspective on the testimony and the theology.

The map of Israel was considerably changed by the Six-Day War and its aftermath, ideologically and politically as well as geographically. Religiously, there has been a shift to the political right; the *kipah serugah*,[51] due to the influence and high visibility of the Active Messianic position, has been more often than before identified with hawkish and maximalist territorial orientations. At the same time, the exhilaration and the sense of new vistas have quite evaporated, and the sense of unity to which many testified in 1967 has been replaced by tension and profound distrust. What, then, remains of the positions that crystallized after the Six-Day War?

The Active Messianic position, as is well known, became the platform of *Gush Emunim*, formally established to 'save the Redemption', as it were, after the setbacks of the 1973 Yom Kippur War. *Gush Emunim* mobilized much religious idealism and won considerable sympathy for the renaissance of 'values' it fortified in the individualistic and even hedonistic society of contemporary Israel. Many saw in them the true heirs of the *halutzim* (the early Jewish pioneers), the only 'real' Zionists left. But *Gush Emunim* also contributed to the alienation of many Israelis from religion. Its identification of Judaism (at least in the public eye) with policies of an aggressive and self-aggrandizing Messianism made adherence to humanistic values look like a secular virtue. Moreover, the discovery of a Jewish terrorist 'underground' in the early 1980s, sprouting from within the settlements and yeshivot of *Gush Emunim*, brought to public awareness that the politics of Messianism could engender violence and brutality as well as 'clean-cut' religious idealism. The 'underground', indeed, led to a soul-searching in *Gush Emunim* itself.

I believe the theological position that hopes for Providential Presence in history without ever taking it for granted may, despite its ambiguities, again become the mainstream stance of religious Zionism, especially in interaction with the position of Moral Halakhism. If it returns to these positions, religious Zionism can maintain a hold both on historical Messianism and on the Zionist present, made holy through halakhic deliberation, critical loyalty and stubborn hope.

As for Position Three – based on the memory of miracles – one may learn from the experience of Elijah that miracles have little staying power. After the fire and after the storm, comes the still small voice that is seldom heard. If this is forgotten, even great miracles may leave no more than an ideological residue of ostrich-like confidence that anything we desire will come to pass no matter what we do. In the decades following the Yom Kippur War, there emerged a kind of *haredi* nationalistic maximalism which found expression in slogans on car stickers: *Yisrael: B'taeh BaShem* (Israel: Put your trust in God), and which was comfortable with the idea that 'the whole world is against us'.

The Moral Halakhism of Position Four was represented by *Oz V'Shalom* and *Netivot Shalom*.[52] If these groups have had little influence it may be because the general (and religious) public could not clearly distinguish their views from those of the secular-minded Peace Now movement, which denied the authority of the sacred tradition and was uninterested in Jewish Messianism as such. (We suggest that those representing this position require dialogue with other religious Jews whose Zionist concerns have theological dimensions, including moderate voices in *Gush Emunim*.)[53]

Position Five, represented by Professor Leibowitz, accurately predicted many of the negative features of redemptive politics in Israel. And yet, situated so idiosyncratically between *Agudat Yisrael* and leftist non-Zionist peace movements, it lost touch with most religious Zionists and others who *did* ascribe spiritual significance to a state for which many gave their lives and who *did* look towards the day when 'the bloody mess of history' becomes, if not the Kingdom of God itself, at least an approach to it.

Position Six, at least in its moderate *Agudist* formulations, gained in influence and strength, and our analysis suggests at least one reason for this is that the *Haredim* have never allowed anyone to draw them into theological discussion. To use Arieli's conception, they knew themselves to be citizens of the past and future and they looked upon loyalists of the present as enemies, knaves and fools. This was not understood by the religious Zionists, who took the present seriously; they considered the *Haredim* as 'really very religious Jews', albeit quaint. Therefore, they remained 'open' to them, vulnerable to their influence especially in the educational institutions of religious Zionism in which their influence grew progressively and generated widespread 'movements of religious return (*teshuva*)' (ostensibly to the sources, but in fact, a strengthening of ultra-Orthodoxy and of its reading of these sources).

When present events and, most particularly, the Six-Day War, appeared to Zionists to be the Messianic future itself, a theological confirmation of the (secular) Zionist ethos, the *Haredim* had only to wait for the enthusiasm to wane and for the hope to fade. Then they could convincingly argue that the enthusiasm was merely another false Messianism – that salvation lay in the past and in the distant future. And with that began the flight, even in *Mizrachi* (religious Zionist) circles, from the challenges of the Zionist present into the citadels of ultra-Orthodoxy, where there were no fighter planes to be manned, no moral problems of statehood to be tackled, no Zionist vision to be realized. *Gush Emunim,* in insisting that the redemption was already here, sounded much less realistic than *Agudat Yisrael.*

Yet one should note that the evacuation of settlers from the Gaza strip in the summer of 2006, constituted an enormous challenge for the settlers, now evicted from their homes and farms. When thousands from throughout the country demonstrably joined these settlers, who were in many senses the major embodiment of religious Zionism, the stage was set for insurrection and violence, against the police and against the army, *their army*. It was a moment of crisis and decision. Crisis – because the text of redemption, of Messianism and of tradition loyal to the Zionist present, seemed blurred and erased: Were these policemen and soldiers the emissaries of God's renewed presence in His land? Decision – because outspoken opposition to the evacuation would have signaled the end of the religious Zionist venture. The people of Gush Katif, as the region of Jewish settlement in Gaza was named, refused, regardless of their political orientation, to shatter the vision. There were scenes of passive resistance to 'their' soldiers and policemen, shows of refusal to evacuate. Many were carried out of their houses. But they kept the process to dimensions of protest. After being forced from their homes, the youth of each place went to their various synagogues to sing and to recite the afternoon prayers, knowing that at dawn, all of these synagogues would be burned to the ground among cheering Palestinian crowds. What transpired there makes me wonder whether a theological vision, too, requires an input of unmediated experience to maintain its vitality, to keep memory alive. In our case it was a lesson taught by religious Zionism, and it must be given its due. After all it is a difficult task to live the tradition, anticipate the coming of the redemption, and not to shirk responsibility for a flawed present, to live and work where the action is.

And yet there are moments of dual meeting, of testimony and theology. The enthusiasm and excitement of the weeks between Independence Day and Shavuot 1967 were appropriate to that time and in that place, despite the pain and bereavement of war. Those who recited the elegy of mourning, *El Male Rachamim*[54] also recited the *Hallel*, and justifiably so. But the experience of these past decades indicates that what is authentic testimony in the flashes of light we call God's Presence, may not be confused, certainly not in our concretely historical Jewish state, with theology and with the life we live as service of God. Good testimony may be bad theology. A living Jewish faith, in Israel as elsewhere, requires both – and the ability to distinguish between them.

1. This essay is based largely on my "Religious Reactions: Testimony and Theology" in Stephen J. Roth (Ed.), *The Impact of the Six-Day War: A Twenty Year Assessment*, London: Macmillan Press in association with the Institute of Jewish Affairs, 1988, pp. 209-231. Published here with permission.

2. Ephraim Yair, *"Yamim gedolim be-Yisrael* (Great Days in Israel)" *Amudim* (Journal of the Religious Kibbutz Movement) 256 (June 1967, Sivan 5727) p. 301.

3. *Siach Lohamim (Soldiers' Talk)*, published by Young Members of the Kibbutz Movement, Tel Aviv, Tishrei 5728, p. 241 (translation mine). For an English edition of *Siach Lohamim*, see Henry Near (trans.), *The Seventh Day: Soldiers Talk About the Six Day War*, Harmondsworth: Penguin, 1971

4. Emil L. Fackenheim, "Jewish Faith and the Holocaust; A Fragment", *Commentary*, 46 (2), (August 1968) p. 86

5. Hanan Porat, *"Ki Ayin B'Ayin Yir'u B'Shuv HaShem Tzion* (With Their Own Eyes They Will See God's Return to Zion)" *Petachim*, 2 (32), Nissan 5735, pp. 9-10

6. Milton Himmelfarb, "In the Light of Israel's Victory", *Commentary*, 44 (4) (October 1967) p. 61

7. A *yeshiva* is an institution of religious study where sacred literature, particularly the Talmud, is studied, often from early youth.

8. Danny Rubenstein, *Mi LaShem Elai: Gush Emunim (On the Lord's Side: Gush Emunim)*, Tel Aviv, 1982, p. 22

9. *Siach Lohamim* (Muki Tzur, "On One of Those Nights") p. 7. This and a number of citations from *Siach Lohamim* and several other sources in the first section of this essay are discussed in my 'Moments of the Heart', *Judaism*, 17 (2) (Spring 1968) pp. 211-24

10. On the basis of a telephone conversation between Mr. Elkins and myself, May 1987. Not only did both networks hold up the story, but the BBC broadcast, when it was finally given, reminded listeners that "the truth is often the first casualty of any war".

11. Eliezer Schweid, *"Yemei Shiva* (Days of Return)" *Petachim*, 1 (1), Tishrai 5725, p. 20. Schweid states that "In the war, the wall of estrangement [of secular youth from the Jewish tradition] seems to have burst".

12. *Siach Lohamim*, p. 232

13. Andre Neher, *"Chizuk Hazehut Hayehudit Al Yedei Ha'avarat Morashto shel Hayehudi Hamoderni'* (Strengthening Jewish Identity Through the Transmission of the Modern Jew's Heritage)" *Bahutzot HaGolah*, 3 (42) (Fall 1967, 5728) pp. 16-21

14. *Siach Lohamim*, p. 40

15. *Amudim* (257-258) (July-August 1967; Tammuz-Av 5727) p. 363

16. *Siach Lohamim,* pp. 21-2

17. *Hashomer Hatzair* – affiliated to the liberal-socialist Mapam

18. Rena Barzilai, "679 Ambassadors" – first published in *The Week in the Kibbutz Ha'Artzi* (September 1967) and frequently reprinted.

19. A *minyan* is a quorum of ten males required for communal prayer. Plural: *Minyanim*

20. Harold Fisch, "Jerusalem, Jerusalem", *Judaism,* 17 (2) (Spring 1968) p. 265.

21. On 'habits of the heart' as a cultural phenomenon, see Robert N. Bellah et al., *Habits of the Heart: Individualism and Commitment in American Life,* Berkeley, 1985, where, following de Tocqueville, they are defined as "notions, opinions and ideas that 'shape mental habits'" and "the sum of moral and intellectual dispositions of men in society".

22. Festival of Light commemorating the successful Maccabean revolt against the Greeks (168-143 BC).

23. Professor Shalom Rosenberg of the Hebrew University, in conversation with the writer.

24. Isaiah Leibowitz, *Ha'Aretz* (30 June 1967) (Hebrew)

25. For an interesting discussion, see Tzuriel Admonit, *"Ha'evkeh... V'al Ma Evkeh?* (Shall I Weep... and About What?)" in Admonit's collected writings, *Betoch Hazerem V'negdo (Within the Stream and Against It),* Tel Aviv, 5737, 428-30

26. A *mitzvah* (plural *mitzvot)* is a religious obligation with the connotation of fulfilling simultaneously both a legal and a moral duty.

27. See Ya'akov Levinger, *"Chiddush Ha'Avodah B'zman Hazeh* (On Renewing the Sacrificial Service in This Era)" *De'ot* (Journal of Religious Academicians) 34 and 35 (Fall and Winter 5728). See also, R. J. Zvi Werblowsky, "The Temple and the Sacrifice", *The Jerusalem Post* (25 August 1967)

28. Nahum Arieli, *"Ha'Ide-a Hatzionit Hadadit – Hatiferet V' Hakishalon* (The Idea of Religious Zionism – The Glory and the Failure)" *Kivvunim*, 29 (Autumn 1985) pp. 25-46

29. See R. J. Zvi Werblowsky, 'Crises of Messianism', *Judaism*, 7 (2) (1958) pp. 106-20

30. Cited in Uriel Tal, "The Land and the State of Israel in Israeli Religious Life", *Proceedings of the Rabbinical Assembly*, 76th Annual Convention, XXXVIII (1976) p. 10

31. Ibid.

32. Ephraim Yair, *Amudim*, 256 (June 1967; Sivan 5727). Yair, though, does concede parenthetically that it may be necessary to relinquish certain heavily-populated territories – but this, he stresses, is a pragmatic necessity and does not undermine the correctness of the theological position.

33. Shubert Spero, "The Religious Meaning of the State of Israel", *Forum*, 24 (1) p. 74. While this position is not necessarily identical or politically in agreement with other forms of Active Messianism (specifically, *Gush Emunim*) it has been placed in this category for its basic orientation that history is being 'changed' by the God of History at present, and that those who understand this will find various events, including the Holocaust, comprehensible as part of a redemptive process which demands the response of recognition and appropriate action.

34. Hanan Porat, *Hatzole* (daily newspaper of the National Religious Party) 2 February 1973.

35. Festival commemorating the saving of Jews from annihilation in ancient Shushan (Persia), as related in the Book of Esther.

36. Yaacov Herzog, "The Meaning of Israel's Resurgence", in *A People That Dwells Alone: Speeches and Writings*, London, 1975, pp. 56-57

37. On the distinction between salvation and redemption, and the requirements of the salvational situation, see also my discussion, "The *Mitzvot*, the Messiah and the Territories", *Tradition*, 10 (3) (Spring 1969), pp. 12-40

38. Cited in Yona Cohen, *"Milchemet Sheshet Hayamim* (The Six-Day War)" in *Shana B'Shana,* Yearbook of Haichal Shlomo (Jerusalem, 5728) pp. 300-301

39. Isaiah 8:11

40. *Hallel* is a prayer recited on celebratory days; on such days which are also marked by tragedy only half the prayer is recited, but in this case, due to the momentousness of the occasion, the Chief Rabbi of Israel declared that the full prayers should be said.

41. During the period between Passover and Shavuot (49 days) all celebrations are forbidden for 33 days (counted differently in different communities). Yet all excluding the Haredi population, accept Lag B'Omer and Jerusalem Day as released from restrictions.

42. Quoted in S. Zalman Abramov, *Perpetual Dilemma: Jewish Religion in the Jewish State,* London UK & Cranbury NJ, USA: Associated University Presses Inc., 1976, p. 247

43. See, for example, Ephraim E. Urbach, *"Aizehu Gibbor? Mi She'ose Son'o Ohavo* (Who is a Warrior? He Who Makes His Enemy Into a Friend)" *Petachim,* 13 (5) (Iyar 5730) pp. 5-8

44. "Peace as a Jewish Value: A Talk With Aviezer Ravitsky", *Oz V'Shalom,* English Bulletin 7-8 (Jerusalem, Fall 1986) pp. 28-29

45. The clan of the Maccabees and their successors, who fought against Hellenization and later, Roman oppression, determined to die rather than yield.

46. A code of Jewish behavior, based on the Talmud, by Joseph Caro, published 1565

47. Isaiah Leibowitz, 'The Spiritual and Religious Meaning of Victory and Might', *Tradition,* 10 (3) 7

48. Agudat Yisrael - political and religious movement which views the Torah as interpreted by traditional commentators as the only legitimate code of laws binding on the Jews and on Israeli society.

49. Two strictly Orthodox anti-Zionist sects.

50. For a detailed discussion, see Norman Lamm, "The Ideology of the Neturei Karta", *Tradition*, 13 (1) pp. 38-53

51. 'Knitted skullcaps' worn by religious Zionists, who have been traditionally in the mainstream of Israeli politics and less militant than the ultra-Orthodox.

52. Two religious peace movements.

53. In the opinion of the writer, who was a member of *Oz V'Shalom*.

54. "God full of Mercy" – prayer of mourning.

IV

Enduring the Silence:
Theology and the Holocaust[1]

In my Introduction, I depicted Theology as the 'field' that examines and describes the relationship between God and humankind, and Jewish theology as examining the relationships and encounters between God and the people of Israel, through the Covenant that the tradition views as Divine-human encounter par excellence.

Some readers may find this rhetoric pompous and bombastic, all the more so as we move to a consideration of the Holocaust. Indeed, here we seem to have reached the end of meaningful and legitimate involvement of theology in our discussion. If the American-Jewish theologian and educator, Irving (Yitz) Greenberg, is correct in stating that no theological discussion is permissible that cannot be conducted in the presence of burning children, then theology has been deprived of a voice in the crucial conversation between God and the Jews and, indeed, all of humanity, with regard to evil, and justice, and covenant.

Yet, while most writers are likely to agree with Greenberg, it is part of the theological method to continue the conversation at any cost in the belief that this will revive theology and, through it, the crucial issues of faith with which theology deals.

However, the issue can be presented as not necessarily theological at all! Indeed, the Holocaust continues to be a prominent feature of contemporary Jewish education, especially secondary education, and 'Holocaust studies' are markedly, some would say disproportionately, represented in Jewish Studies programs at universities around the world. So one could also view this emphasis on study of the Holocaust as a response to the religious diversity and disunity among Jews. One may argue that since the Holocaust struck indiscriminately at all varieties of believers and non-believers, the study of it may arouse a consciousness of ethnic commonalities among Jews without demanding religious conformity or even a common religious consciousness among them. Ironically, such a manifestly ethnic-historical approach to the Holocaust seems to solve the problem of 'how to keep away from theology' while not staying studiously away from the Holocaust itself, even allowing for historical study of religious consciousness during the Holocaust as an important topic of Jewish and universal concern.

Theology, Despite All That

Yet for many, the theological dimension remains the crucial one, despite the difficulties it confronts in the face of unmitigated evil. How may one think about the relationship with God when He is so manifestly absent?

Approaches to this question are varied. Some declare that the Holocaust requires a ringing reaffirmation of traditional doctrines and persuasive presentations of traditional theodicies to the (potentially) questioning young; others say that the Great Destruction obliges even committed Jews to re-examine everything they believed or thought they knew about God, humankind and Judaism. They maintain that if Jews are to have any continuity of faith or at least of identity after the Holocaust, they must honestly rethink the doctrinal and symbolic world of their tradition. Some go further and say, "The Torah was given at Sinai and returned at Lublin". [2] Jewish realms of meaning are no longer accessible to us.

Five Theological Orientations

In addition to 'ethnic' or national approaches to Holocaust consciousness and teaching, then, for which issues of faith are peripheral or totally irrelevant, there are also theological approaches for which these issues are focal. I shall look briefly at five major theological orientations. One of these sees no need for theological re-thinking, and denies that God was in any sense absent or 'silent' during the Holocaust years. The other four take cognizance of Divine 'silence'. Here are the various positions on a theological continuum.

1 – In the first view, *"Nothing is wrong at all in the relationship between God and Israel"*. While much is awry with the contemporary world and with Jews who have fallen under its pernicious sway, the classic teachings regarding divine Providence – including the doctrine of retribution for transgression – are, if anything, vindicated by the

horrendous events. Three variations on this theological position should be mentioned:

(a) Israel is said to be suffering for its sins, whether they be a falling away from religious observance and commitment and the idolatrous trust in Zionism, or conversely, Israel is being punished for its 'rebellious' refusal to return to the Land of Israel in this redemptive age. Having embraced secular nationalism and socialism, say disciples of this school of thought, Jews should not be surprised that God has ironically made the (Nazi) National-Socialists the rod of His wrath.[3]

(b) Another view within this orientation has it that the people of Israel is the 'suffering servant', the victim of humanity's crimes; a suffering imposed on them in order to bring about some redemptive or even Messianic 'turn' in human history. It is thus providential that after the Holocaust, the State of Israel, 'the beginning of our redemption', was established. A related view: both the world and Israel were purified for the coming of redemption. Those terrible days of suffering and abandonment are best described as "the birth pangs of the Messiah".[4]

(c) The Holocaust is not only a great punishment but a series of great miracles (vouchsafed to righteous individuals) in the midst of the cataclysm. These miracles reflect on the merits of specific righteous individuals on the one hand, and on their being God's instruments in furthering His purpose for Israel, on the other. While His justice will be done, His love for Israel requires both the survival of selected faithful persons and the maintenance of fervent faith throughout the community of "the righteous remnant".[5]

2 – A second orientation has it that *"Something is wrong"*. There is a flaw in the present Jewish-Divine relationship; we find ourselves distant from the biblical ideal of covenantal encounter and intimacy. For the Covenant promises that the commanding God is also the God of our salvation. In the Holocaust world, this saving God was silent. Consequently, all attempts to fathom the meaning of the Holocaust, for example, by interpreting the catastrophe as Divine retribution for transgression, are ludicrous and even blasphemous. They are ludicrous because there was not and could never be enough sinfulness to justify such a punishment, and blasphemous because a God who would punish one million children by torturing, gassing and burning them deserves neither loving reverence nor devoted service, and one who describes God thus, is defaming Him. However, according to this approach, although we cannot explain, we are to respond to the events. In Fackenheim's celebrated formulation, though there was no "saving Presence" at Auschwitz, there was a "commanding Presence" that spoke the "six hundred and fourteenth commandment" obliging Jews to survive. The people of Israel were commanded not to give Hitler 'posthumous victories' by abandoning Judaism, its people and its God.[6]

Also within this orientation we find such Orthodox positions as Norman Lamm's.[7] Lamm admits to the unavailability of divine meaning, but categorizes it as divine eclipse, *hester Panim,* which denotes "God's self-removal from the context of Israel's company into His transcendence and remoteness". *Hester Panim,* says Lamm, began with the destruction of the Second Temple, and since then "there is no clear 'sense' or 'meaning' in Jewish history." Such absence, Lamm insists, is not intrinsic, but historical: it has a beginning point and it is hopefully drawing to a close. The (perhaps!) redemptive events of Israel's re-emergence, may indicate *nesiat Panim,* God's "lifting of His face" in love and devotion. But in any case, the way of religious response is prescribed: "It may be more difficult to pray (in a state of *hester Panim*) but pray we must. It may seem impossible to feel His presence, but feel we must as we bend all our energies and innermost emotions to His service."

3 – According to a third theological option *"Something* (only) *seems to be wrong".* The character of our tradition is such that encountering unexplainable situations creates a crisis of faith. This mandates a restatement of Judaism's fundamentally halakhic theological principles. When the response demanded by the situation is understood, the crisis is overcome and God's voice is again heard – from within the pristine Torah tradition.

The theological positions within this orientation are generally presented as traditional doctrine. Thus Eliezer Berkovits,[8] while agreeing that no 'answer' emerged from the Holocaust that might explain it, yet places this silence within a framework of theodicy. God's silence is an essential and perennial prerequisite of human freedom which would be neutralized by constant divine intervention in history.

His theological hero is the Tannaic (second century) sage, Rabbi Akiba who, as he was being flayed to death by the Romans, recited the *Shema*. Guided by his halakhic perspective, Berkovits insists that Rabbi Akiba did this not for innovative dramatic effect, but rather for the explicit halakhic reason that the particular moment of his flagellation was "the prescribed time for saying the *Shema*". Through his very commandedness, Rabbi Akiba stood in encounter with the commanding God, above the event. Like the Holocaust victim who was able to 'brush off' his oppressors, by musing or exclaiming "Let them go to hell!", so Rabbi Akiba was too engaged with the mitzvah of reciting the *Shema* at its proper time to 'pay attention', as it were, to his torturers and killers. They were extrinsic elements in a situation that gave him the 'privilege' of "loving God with all your soul" in the manner that he himself had interpreted the verse: "Even when He takes your soul".

In the writings of Rabbi J.B. Soloveitchik,[9] the inability of mortals to understand the meaning of events and even a kind of indifference to such meanings is given perennial halakhic status and sanction. The Halakhah, Soloveitchik insists, demands *response* to evil, not futile attempts to understand it. Similarly, for the scholar and thinker, Isaiah Leibowitz,[10] the halakhic framework of response or "service of God" is the sum total of Judaism's communal face, though the individual may achieve (intellectually oriented) "love of God".[11] Leibowitz interprets this love as seeking and gaining a pristine understanding of what is determined and can be known in the human world (i.e., the world open to research) as well as what can be

Michael Rosenak

experienced as non-determined in human existence, and can be 'religiously' experienced. For Leibowitz, then, the cardinal symbol of Judaism is the *Akedah*, the sacrifice of Isaac, representing Abraham's readiness to give all for God, in contradistinction to symbols like the (Christian) cross which point to God's alleged nurturing love and self-sacrifice on behalf of humanity.

4 – According to a fourth approach, *"Something is indeed radically wrong"*. God's silence during the Holocaust is inexplicable and threatens the entire structure of Jewish faith. Before there can be the cultural re-affirmation that contemporary Judaism vitally needs, there must be thorough re-thinking. Only then can religious renewal perhaps become feasible.

In the previous orientations, all 'answers' (1) and all 'responses' (2-3) have theological and midrashic precedents. They are part of what Fackenheim has called "the midrashic framework".[12] Other thinkers, however, insist that certain central features of classic Jewish doctrine may have to be explicitly jettisoned after the Holocaust in order to make space for the intellectual, moral and perhaps even religious rehabilitation of the rest.

Eliezer Schweid[13] has extensively spelled out this view. He maintains that religious faith in a covenantal relationship constitutes a moral stance that ultimately stands or falls on reciprocity between the Divine and humans, who choose to engage and absolutely trust in one another. In times of crisis, the human partners to the Covenant look back reflectively at historical antecedents and attempt to incorporate the present crisis into the tapestry of tradition. In such reflection, they cannot avoid asking what is demanded of both partners to the Covenant. What God demands, so tradition and historical narratives dictate, is righteousness (*zedek*), and *zedakah* is what is due the righteous one – what God 'owes' him or her who absolutely trusts Him. When the human being does not receive the *zedakah* he or she has the right to expect, the *zedek* demanded by God and 'owed' Him, becomes implausible. Then the consciousness of historical tradition that seeks to mend each breach by recalling past love, trust and reciprocity cannot be sustained. The greater the seeming injustice of God, the greater the challenge to the moral balance of faith.

This position makes no covenantal sense to Schweid. Either God is seen to love the people of Israel who have undertaken to love Him, or the Covenant must ultimately be called into question. Hence Schweid draws the conclusion that the traditional faith in historical Providence, especially against the backdrop of modern civilization, is no longer automatic. Indeed it seems no longer tenable.

5 – A fifth position maintains that the *entire theological enterprise of Judaism is wrong.* The two positions alluded to above, that which sees in response, halakhic or otherwise, the very essence of contemporary (even perennial) Jewish theology, and that which in opposition to this argues that parts of the tradition may have to be called seriously into question in this historical hour, are both thoroughly radicalized in the non-theistic theology of Richard Rubenstein.[14] He insists that no meaning can be mined from

the traditional world picture of Judaism, and its divine 'first actor'. If we accept that the mythic world of classic Judaism is false, then God is not silent, but 'dead'. Yet, in a world devoid of divinity, the significance of Torah grows as a system of communal patterns and rituals in which Jews may 'huddle together' in a hostile cosmos. One is, in a sense, no less intensely commanded by the haplessness of human existence than by the traditional Deity. The leaders who structure this cultural existence are restored to their primordial priestly status. But the message of the prophets, who claimed to speak for a moral Commander, is exposed by the Holocaust to be illusionary. In a world of continuous upheaval and growing chaos, this illusion is a dangerous and potentially fatal one.

Teaching and Education

Here, then, are some of the options available to the teacher for whom Holocaust instruction, no matter what else it may be, is also a theologically-conscious enterprise for transmitting new and presumably more feasible theology to children in the post-Holocaust age. For those in Jewish education will always ask themselves: what do we want our children to think and believe about God and the Jewish people? Conversely, some of these approaches might indeed, singly or in combination, buttress traditional beliefs in an age of secular anarchy.

But is theology necessary at all in more than the strictly instructional sense that it might be worth some lessons on contemporary Jewish thought? As we have seen, this question characterizes adherents of the ethnic-national approach. They insist that what Jews believed is only one, even minor element in a rational understanding of what transpired. More important were the socio-economic crisis into which Europe was moving before the Hitler era that swept Jews into its juggernaut; the anomalous position of Jews among the peoples of the world; and the relentless force of Christian and post-Christian anti-semitism. Is such an approach not more reasonable? Does not theology as a 'world view' that permeates educational institutions, inevitably tailor facts to suit its heresies or theodicies? Is it not indoctrination, divisive and polemical? Should subject-matter not expand both knowledge and understanding? Can theology do that?

These are all powerful arguments but, of course, ethnic-national positions such as these also reflect and favor a specific world-view. They too have an explicit or implicit view of what constitutes valuable knowledge and what it means to 'understand' things. Their world-view is based on the assumption that Jewish existence is best approached as would any other; that classic Jewish self-understanding as covenantal is presumptuous and largely irrelevant. In line with this view, Jewish problems become amenable to solution only when they are de-mystified. Theology, if taken too seriously, is thus part of the very problem to be solved!

Educational Visions and Educational Theories

For our discussion, there is much insight to be gained from the 'ethnic' approach. Moreover it illustrates the fact that there is no agreed upon 'Holocaust education'. Witness the fact that even knowledgeable teachers, who have mastered and conscientiously teach reliable data about the Shoah, may actually still be educating to any one of such beliefs, sentiments and valuative prescriptions as:

a) sensitivity to social and moral wrongs and the ability to identify socio-economic forces that may, with intelligence, be (partially) controlled;

b) a rejection of the idea of divine Providence in understanding our lives and planning our futures;

c) distrust of other nations: trusting 'only ourselves';

d) a resolve never to forget or forgive the Nazi Amalekites;

e) a conviction that human life has no intrinsic value but can yet be lived heroically;

f) a belief that God's ways are inscrutable, together with gratitude for our lives and the continued existence of our people, now miraculously restored to its homeland;

g) the certainty that the Holocaust was punishment for our sins;

h) pride at the transformation of the Jews from the status of pitiful victims to proud self-defenders, coupled with trepidation lest strength lead to brutalization and cruelty.

Now, in fact, the Holocaust by itself does not 'teach' these things, which are partially mutually contradictory and largely moot. What the Holocaust 'teaches' does not flow inexorably from 'the facts' but from open or hidden agendas which foster a vision of the educated person; a vision that, in turn, is based on given philosophical principles. These agendas are transmitted, even by conscientious and knowledgeable teachers, through diverse ways of selecting from subject matter, organizing it, making or withholding emphases, accompanying it by tones of voice and conscious or unconscious body language. Education is done by teachers and by those who decide on Shoah Memorial Day television presentations, by the rabbis, historians and film-makers who are acknowledged to be experts and who present extracurricular activities on the subject with the consent and blessing of the community and the school, as well as by those who determine when sirens shall be sounded and "minutes of silence" observed.

The educational issues raised are not exclusive to Holocaust education, but they pertain to Holocaust education in particular as this is a subject that theologically cannot be taught if uninformed by vision and humility, on the one hand, and mindful concern for the diverse educational perspectives, on the other. This requires stepping back from the subject, even while confronting it.

Teaching, in and of itself, aims to impart organized knowledge, for enlightenment and for use. But teaching is also founded on a vision of ideal human beings. Educational visions, of course, are various. Some have clear-cut, even rigid, social ideals and socializing agendas. Others see social habit as a mere prelude to the individual judgment that must be exercised as soon as the psychological facts of human development make it possible. Some visions are fundamentally secular; they place value-making societies and individuals at the center of the human enterprise.

Others are religious, locating the significance of human life and society in encounter with divinity, however understood. Most traditionally-oriented educational visions tend to be normative, emphasizing the commanded or duty-oriented character of the good life. Conversely, many modern conceptions are experimental or deliberative. They portray the educated person as capable of locating problems and competent to seek, formulate and implement appropriate solutions to them.

Educational visions are not merely variegated but also competitive and often conflicting. And in the often polemical conversation among educational philosophies, the following questions inevitably arise:

(1) Does a particular vision permit or encourage an imbalance between constituent elements of the educational situation? Is there too much – or too little – emphasis on society or on the subject matter (what is ostensibly being learned), the teacher or the learner? Has a particular approach perhaps defined these terms in arbitrary ways in order to disguise the imbalance among them? For example, are learners perceived merely as those 'being initiated into community'?[15]

(2) Have particular competing visions, because they grant educational monopolies to, say, moralistic subject matter, or to 'the child', removed themselves from the realm of education and crossed the line into indoctrination, or therapy, or anarchy? For example, has educational success been defined exhaustively as loyalty, health, or freedom?[16]

(3) Can a particular competing vision actually be translated from the realm of abstract principle to that

of concrete practice? For example, how will a secular-existential approach that denies the status of heteronymous absolutes and demands choice-making of its ideally educated person, cope with the psychological need for certainties and the consequent tendency of secularized individuals and nations to "escape from freedom" – into fundamentalism and totalitarianism? Conversely, can a religiously-grounded educational vision make room for social and individual diversity, and individual autonomy? And should it?

In order to translate educational visions into educational theories that can guide concrete practice, educators must respond to each of these challenges for themselves. Thus:

(a) Educators should clarify, on principled grounds, the relationships they recommend between the various elements of education. If they give a preeminent place to a particular 'element' (such as subject matter or the teacher), they should justify, in terms of their vision and the vision's underlying philosophy, why they do so.

(b) Educators should explicate their view of what 'education' is and what is meant by 'succeeding' at it. In some cases this will involve legitimating what others have ruled out. For example, Catholic or ultra-Orthodox Jewish educators may insist that indoctrination is not antithetical to 'good' education, no matter what heretics say. In other cases, they will redefine the offensive category. For example, they may stipulate that 'indoctrination' is the teaching of false doctrines that limit growth 'as we define growth'.

(c) Educators should deliberate on the concrete difficulties of translating philosophical educational visions into theories that guide practice. For example: a particular educator may accept the psychological position that children become 'open' adults if they have been introduced into a world that is basically friendly.[17] In this approach they grapple with ways to envision the educational negotiation between the perceived reality of a largely hostile world on the one hand and an orientation of 'friendliness' on the other hand, without simply lying to children.

Here we have raised some pristine questions. Now let us add the element of theology into our deliberations.

Truthful Theologies and Educated Jews

The seeming digression below is meant to enrich and balance our discussion of the theological dimension of teaching the Holocaust, particularly in religious Jewish education. It suggests that the enterprise of teaching the Holocaust is only a subject-matter component of a larger educational domain; a domain that, for religiously-minded educators, is a crucial one. (We should, of course, remember that the Holocaust raises educational problems and perplexities in addition to theological ones. Though theology can help us to deal with these educational issues, at times it may exacerbate our problems.)

We must realize that the contemporary theological approaches to the Holocaust that educators have at their disposal are not simply material that can be judged in terms of educational impact. First and foremost, theologically-oriented religious educators who confront theologies – both as bodies of principle that shape their visions and as 'subject-matter' that transmits competence and wisdom – have to consider the *truthfulness*, the *coherence* and *plausibility* of the theological propositions being placed before them. Only then can they examine whether the educational ideals and practices that flow from them are congenial ones.

By *truthfulness* we refer not to the demonstrated propositional truth of the theological position under consideration. Rather we have in mind the trust of its recipients in the spiritual integrity of those who present it. We are thinking, also, of the ability and willingness of these who study it to 'find' it in their religious experience and behavior: the theology in question 'rings a bell'. It is illuminating and is worth thinking through. It is capable of teaching something about the non-intellectual aspects of religious life. Thus it suggests reasons (*taamim*) and avenues of significance for the observance of commandments, singly and as a whole.

By *coherence* I refer to the requirement that diverse features or propositions of the theological position not contradict one another. Though there may be paradoxes among them due to the 'depth' of the objects of theological discourse (God, the human soul, the text as a pointer to ultimacy), they yet support one another and 'come together' in some way.

By *plausibility* I have in mind the possibility of explaining a conception, at least partially, to an outsider. Such a person will be enabled to 'get the drift' of the position, and to see the sense in it without necessarily accepting it or agreeing with it. If plausibility is applied, it dissipates the seeming arbitrariness.

Now, when educators turn their attention to the relationship between educational ideals and the concrete problems of practice in the teaching of the Holocaust, they may find certain options, though theologically acceptable, to exact a heavy educational price; others, seemingly sound from an educational standpoint, will be judged as theologically unacceptable.

Let us illustrate the tension that may arise between theological acceptability and educational feasibility.

A theological approach that sees no problem in principle with a retributive God who punishes the wicked *and* the hapless righteous caught in the maelstrom but Who yet performs miracles in line with His power and His purpose can be deemed truthful by Jews immersed in Bible and Midrash. They may even plausibly explain that "My (i.e., God's) thoughts are not your thoughts" (Isaiah 55:8). Yet, on the plane of educational vision, this approach fosters an ideal of the educated Jew whose God is powerful and even present, but 'silent' while babies are killed and saints are tortured. Being less than an Isaiah, can a Jew envision such a God as other than cruel? Would the Jew who believes this, trust a mortal friend who behaved like that?! Does this not raise problems of coherence for the theology itself?[18] Because this approach is so scantly plausible, it may cogently be argued that it is practically feasible only within the omnipresent, compact and secluded community of the faithful, that imposes its view of reality unambiguously upon its children. Though in its own eyes an exemplary model of unperturbed faith, it looks to outsiders like unmitigated socialization, for all other elements of the educational process are consciously subjugated to the societal one. Teachers are socializing agents of community; and subject matter is tailored to what the community's leaders find appropriate. As for children, they are no more than potential 'community members in good standing'. Most educators will argue that that state of society – and of mind – can be achieved only through an education that indoctrinates.

We may say that a theology that completely skirts the problem of God's silence, or serenely accepts it as a given, suggests a character ideal that sacrifices religious significance on the altar of religious obligation. If all religious education is initiation into normative commitment coupled with a principled denial of new significance-bearing Presence, then religious life may well be existentially heroic for the sophisticated, but for most others, it is likely to be a regimen of empty, albeit stubbornly maintained, rote and routine.

In both of these cases, the theologies seem feasible, at least within the context of communal loyalty, but the educational ideals that accompany them seem to be missing something essential. In the first case, the individual as the potential 'address' for singular religiosity has been lost, except for leaders who justify their individuality as required by their community roles. In the second case, the element of religious hope has been overpowered by a theology of stoic acceptance of present reality, of 'trust' within the world as it is.

On the other hand, there are theological positions that appear, at least initially, as educationally edifying but, despite traditional credentials, are theologically problematic. For example, the view that the Holocaust is integral to a process of redemption seems religiously incoherent when it emanates from liberals like Ignatz Maybaum[19] no less than when it comes from traditionalists. One may grasp the idea of historical cataclysm as the act of blind and deterministic forces. But to associate it with the God of compassion, Who ostensibly purified the world and His people through massive death, can only be coherent and (somewhat) plausible when immediately followed by a Messianic Age in which the incomprehensible is fully explained and the dead rise. Yet one hears seemingly plausible arguments for its educational worth. It is said to place the young ideologically in a world that 'makes sense,' that is thick with meaning and 'values'. It anchors their idealism and ideals. It comfortably places even revolutionary change within a Classical framework of significance and obligation. Though firmly located within community, the educated Jew that emerges is not devoid of individuality. Yet, we may comment that he or she is mainly an eschatological figure. His or her faith is all hope transfigured into confidence. Trustful acceptance, then, is replaced by anticipation, and religious responsibility threatens to become simple 'activism'.

The educator who considers theological issues to be germane or crucial to his or her educational project, will therefore have to address two interlocking issues:

(a) What do I (or 'we') believe? What should, then, be the ideational guideposts for Jewish faith even (or especially) after the Holocaust? Who is the God I ideally envision children 'meeting' and 'serving' in their lives? What, therefore, should ideally be presented to children, and at which stage of their development? What, in principle, are the curricular foci and emphases called for?

(b) How is theology, in the wake of the Holocaust, part of educational theory and practice? For example: which data are tolerable, at which stages of education, in which settings? How can the children in my charge learn to relate to God? How, on the basis of what we know of such things, may I envision this relationship evolving as the children mature?

These are specifically educational questions that pinpoint the role of theology in education.

An Illustrative Conception for Modern Religious Education: A Theological Paradigm

So far, we have attempted to cover a large field for purposes of mapping. Now we shall focus specifically upon religious Jewish education which is open to the modern world, interacts with it and learns from it. We suggest four premises in approaching 'the theological dimension' for this type of education:

1 – "The seal of the Almighty is truth" (B.T. Shabbat 55a). The educational project may not bear false witness in order seemingly to *protect* religious faith and practice. Falsehood will ultimately block whatever paths of communication between human beings and the Divine are being 'protected'

or that may yet emerge. "This is my salvation, that the hypocrite cannot come before Him" (Job 13:16).

2 – Religious faith is legitimately challenged, sometimes severely, by 'epoch-making events' but it is founded upon 'root experiences'. Hence religious faith and life may at times change perspectives and sensibilities, for epoch-making events require the creation and internalization of new midrash. Nonetheless, such events reveal no new Torah that supplants that of Sinai. Lublin is a heart-wrenching crisis and catastrophe in Jewish life but it is not a new revelation that mandates discarding the previous one.[20]

3 – The educational transmission of theological content, whether in teaching or as a factor in establishing educational principles and ideals, is fraught with dangers. First, there is the constant pitfall of tendentiousness and apologetics, and hence, of tailoring data in a manner that blatantly hides facts and cultivates legends. Second, there is the temptation to present theology as synonymous with the religious life as a whole rather than a reflection-of-commitment upon it and an intellectual component of it. Hence, within the paradigm of faith, there is always more than one theological option. Getting learners to appreciate that is one of the primary educational reasons for incorporating 'Jewish Thought (*Machshevet Yisrael*)' in the curriculum, and for frequently examining educational visions for an unwanted accruement of dogmatism.

4 – Since theology is only one, perhaps secondary, component of religious life **as it is lived**, the enterprise of 'getting ideas across' to children is legitimately qualified

by other, more primary features of that religious life. For example, not every pedagogic device or 'technique' for bringing the Holocaust 'home' to children and for theologically interpreting it is halakhically acceptable. The exhibition of lampshades made of human tissue or video presentations of piles of corpses raise serious questions with regard to "the dignity of the deceased (*k'vod hamet*)" and the humility demanded of the living.

In addition to specific and clearly delimited halakhic qualifications that religious life imposes upon instruction, there are some that arise out of moral, existential and spiritual considerations that may or may not have been given explicit halakhic formulation. Hence, for educational and religious reasons that precede and transcend the Holocaust and whatever 'lessons are to be learned from it', modern Jewish educators should not draw such conclusions from the Holocaust as (a) one should, in principle, seek to kill all Germans, or (b) brute force is the underlying reality of human existence.

Similarly, inviting a denial of God, for example, by dramatically rehearsing the facts of the Holocaust in contexts wherein children are emotionally vulnerable, even if done only for didactic and heuristic purposes, should not be viewed as admissible in religious education, modern or not.

Trust and Hope

The last point we should like to raise here is the overarching principle, as already intimated above, that a religious educational vision looks towards 'educated persons' who have not been deprived of either trust or hope. By *trust*, I mean the ability of the religious person to 'make do' with the spirituality in the world as it is; by *hope*, the ability to dream, to work at repair, to glimpse a different world wherein the Kingdom of Heaven will be manifest.

These two aspects of religious personality are reflected in the theological realm, among other things, by the categories of the 'hidden' *(nistar)* miracle in contradistinction to the 'open' and self-evident one *(galui).* The person who is attentive to 'hidden miracles' can encounter God everywhere. These miracles remind us of what we have already been given; they may teach us to experience the world as less threatening and, therefore, enable us to live more morally and responsibly in the world as it is.

'Self-evident miracles' as a theological datum address a problem that 'hidden' ones try to transcend or ignore, namely, that the reality of human life is often so hopeless that simply 'encountering God everywhere', while spiritually heroic and intellectually plausible (to some), may be morally outrageous. Where was the concealed miracle for the Israelite parent seeing his or her child replacing mortar or bricks in the crevices of buildings in Pitam and Ramses, or for the twentieth century Jew whose baby was being bayoneted and thrown into a gas chamber? There are times when only an "open" miracle, anticipated and remembered, may restore hope that matters can – and actually will – become different, even as it cannot undo the actual evils endured by humans.

Trust without hope, represented by an exclusivity of hidden miracles, can make children moral yet stoical. They may become serene in an imperfect and often horrific world, and thus unfeeling and complacent. The remembrance of overt miracles must be invoked wherever appropriate (certainly at a Seder!) to engender disquiet and pain vis-à-vis the world as we often find it.

Conversely, hope without trust, that blurs sensitivity to concealed miracles and sees evidence of self-evident miracles around every corner, engenders boundless hope. It is not only unrealistic but destroys faith in the voice that even in hours of silence, may be heard within the reality in which we live. It leads readily to ethical obtuseness to what is going on now and that demands our moral attention. It also paves a road to false Messianism.

Self-evident miracles are unreliable moral guides and they may suggest hopes that are far too narrow. Even at the Passover Seder, Jews customarily remove a drop of wine from their goblets for each plague visited upon the Egyptians, even though these plagues were an element in Israel's redemption! After all, people suffered and died! If moral sensitivity is lost due to an excess of hope, what will become of trust which is built upon sensitivity to what is 'concealed'?

Translating from Theology into Education

We have seen that there are tensions between subject matter 'fields' such as theology, on the one hand, and education on the other, the latter as a domain of principled conceptions and 'visions', and as a practical endeavor guided by didactic, psychological, sociological theories. Education, we find, has a 'language' that permits both philosophical reflection on its goals and the use of theories to shape and re-shape its practice. Hence subject matters which it uses to form its vision and which it incorporates in instruction require translation into educational ideals that picture ideally educated persons. These, in turn, must be translated into theories of pedagogical, psychological or sociological prescriptions for educational action that give the vision a chance of realization.

'Trust' and 'hope' are clearly two facets of an educational conception of an ideal. Namely, if we are dealing with a certain school of religious Jewish educators – those who are also modern in conviction, experience and temperament – we shall generally find them upholding the view that religious personalities ideally internalize both of these religious characteristics. As said, these are educational ideals, and they invite application in educational practice. But we have taken care to relate them to theological categories, namely to hidden and self-evident miracles respectively, which tie specific character ideals to beliefs we hold, or are teaching in the name of a truth. Theology here serves to justify and clarify what educators affirm should be done and what they attempt to actually achieve. Taken by themselves, educational theories, with their frames of reference in social sciences and their educational visions that focus on the educated person, may seem reductionistic, but they are not ever 'taken by themselves'. They are anchored in philosophy, in scientific inquiry, in culture and religion: in 'subject-matter' of various kinds.

Theological Homilies

I shall illustrate translation from theology to education that is congenial to the premises of modern religious education, by thinking through several theological homilies and lessons. These are, of course, not the only theological approaches that are appropriate both to our premises and to the requirement that theology be arguably truthful, coherent and plausible. Nor do they have a monopoly on educational usefulness. But they are illustrative of encounters between Jewish theology and Jewish education.

We begin with a theological lesson on a Scriptural passage by the French-Israeli theologian, Andre Neher.[21] His text is Ezekiel 20 which relates how, in Babylonian exile, "certain of the elders of Israel came to inquire of the Lord". Yet God instructs the prophet to dismiss their request. "Are you come to inquire of Me? As I live, saith the Lord God, I will not be inquired of by you." Neher's midrashic lesson takes its cue from Rashi's commentary to 20:1:

> They came to inquire of the Lord out of their own interest. 'If He refuses to listen to us, well, He will no longer have any claim upon us. A slave sold by his master, a wife driven out by her husband, are they not free of their responsibilities to one another?'

Neher suggests that the elders are seeking a final disposition of the Covenant and that they accept God's speech of dismissal and refusal to 'be "inquired of" by them' with relief. If God is finished with us, so be it. We are freed, then, from the bonds of Covenant. And Neher pictures them as leaving the prophet's presence forthwith.

Then, strangely, there is a long tirade, wherein God recounts Israel's sinfulness in tedious detail. "And when the Preacher returns to His original thought in verse 31, and again insists on His refusal of counsel ('And I, shall I be inquired of by you? No, I will not be inquired of by you!') He, as it were, suddenly notices that His listeners have gone, that they have long since paid heed to His first admonition..." Neher sees the prophet as told to run into the street to bring them back, to 'take them by the scruff of the necks and forcefully regain their attention'. They are forced to listen to God's new word, contrary to His previous outburst. "So you think yourselves free? As I live, saith the Lord God, surely with a mighty hand and with an outstretched arm, and with fury poured out, will I be King over you." (20:33).

It is as though the 'Doctor', in refusing to receive the patient, had prescribed for him the correct remedy... as though the Master, in withdrawing Himself in silence, had imparted the true word to His disciple.

But how can that be? How does silence instruct? Why not simply have the patient tell that strange and seemingly heartless Doctor that he is finished with Him? What prevents that response?

Part of the answer is doubtlessly in the ludicrousness of the situation. Anyone who turns to the Source of his or her identity and asks that Source whether one may relinquish the identity, is certain to be rebuked, brushed off, and laughed at. 'If you wished to lose your identity, would you come to Me? Your turning to Me is itself an affirmation of your identity! As long as you know who you are, "I shall be king over you".'

Terms of reference such as 'identity' are perhaps too overtly 'educational' for Neher. And he suggests a further interpretation as to who these "certain elders of Israel" are, on the basis of a midrash to the Song of Songs (*Shir Hashirim Rabbah* 8:13). This midrash teaches that the men who came to consult God are Hananiah, Mishael and Azariyah, the companions of Daniel called into exile by the Babylonian king, Nebuchadnezzar, to stand in waiting upon him. The king has warned them that if they refuse to worship his idol, they will be cast into a fiery furnace (Daniel 3:15). He taunts them: "Who is the God that will deliver you out of my hands?" and they answer, with seemingly untroubled certainty, that their God will deliver them. Now, seized by anxiety, they come before the prophet to seek reassurance that God will indeed save them. But when the prophet brings their request before God, He startlingly spurns the request: "No, I will not deliver them." The prophet weeps and laments. He reminds God that these are the last of the righteous of Judah, but to no avail. God remains silent. And when the three ask Ezekiel what God has replied, the answer is: "He will not deliver you." And this word of silence creates a new insight and commitment, a new response, a new situation. "Very well, then," they respond, "whether He delivers us or not, we are ready for martyrdom." Neher finds the proof text for that response in Daniel 3:18, where Hananiah, Mishael and Azariyah cast at

Michael Rosenak

Nebuchadnezzar the eternal challenge of the martyrs, *hen-lo*, 'despite all'.

> If that God Who is ours and Whom we serve will not deliver us, despite all of this (*hen-lo*) be it known unto thee, O king, that we will not serve thy gods, nor worship the golden image that thou hast set up.

And Neher comments: "... *hen-lo*, a contradictory formula, is nothing else than the juxtaposition of 'yes' and 'no'. But whereas elsewhere this juxtaposition would be a sign of indecision, of equivocation, of balancing of 'yes' and 'no' leading to a neutral passivity, here it is the supreme symbol of voluntary action, of deliberate and irreversible choice."[22] Whether 'yes, He is close', or 'no, He is silent and remote', we shall serve Him.

Several elements of Neher's theological lesson are striking. First, he views God's silence, the refusal to "be inquired of", as a form of speech, a demand that the human 'listener to silence' be galvanized to a response which changes the situation, or perhaps creates a new religious situation. Neher suggests that martyrdom begins in the assumption that God will not save (even in the case of Daniel's friends, who ultimately were saved). Prior to that 'silence', the religious response, while perhaps worthy, is not – martyrdom. Secondly, at the moment of silence one may anticipate God's speech and that speech may come when no one wishes to listen. Having refused to be inquired of, God immediately presents a case for His previous silence, and demands to rule Israel "with a strong hand". Third, we may note that

Neher chooses to discuss inquirers who certainly have had prior experience of God's speech. These, after all, are the very young men who would not eat the non-kosher food at the king's table (Daniel 1). And, if they had no trust in God and His prophet, why would Daniel's companions go to the prophet to find His re-assuring word? Moreover, where did Hananiah, Mishael and Azariyah find the confidence with which they initially confront Nebuchadnezzar?

Yet even for the prophet who cajoles and laments, God is inscrutable. Sometimes He is present and other times He is not. Though His absences are also 'speech', because the silence creates the space for human activity in ways we may not yet fathom. The reasons God gives for His silence – specifically, that Israel has deserted Him – don't apply to these young men, "the last three righteous of Judah". And while the answer that 'silence is just what they need' may make theological sense, it is not consoling. We are returned to Lamm's insistence that "eclipse" is painful, and demanding; it is accompanied by what Fackenheim calls the "commanding Presence".

Elizabeth Shanks,[23] reflecting on several Talmudic passages, presents a not dissimilar conception. She cites the argument between R. Yochanan in the name of R. Shimon b. Yehozadak and R. Ishmael at the council of Lydda as to whether idolatry belongs, along with unmandated bloodshed and forbidden sexual relationships, in the category of "Allow yourself to be killed rather than transgress" (Sanhedrin 74a). The question is whether one is obligated to give one's life rather than worship idols, or whether this prohibition

171

belongs with all those commandments that do not demand this. Of the latter, Scripture is found to say, "And you shall live by them" (the commandments), i.e., not die by them. The ruling of the Sages is that *public* idolatry does belong to the absolutely forbidden category, in line with the commandment, "Neither shall ye profane My name, but I shall be hallowed among the children of Israel".

Shanks sees this discussion as a rational deliberation about what constitutes an utterly perverted relationship with God, a distortion of the Divine image. The loss of one's life is justified, indeed required, when one risks using one's life to diminish God within this world. But the very rationality of the debate and the assumption that the community is a believing one (that should not have its belief undermined by members who succumb to idolatry in the public sphere) indicate God's presence. Both the sages and R. Ishmael "understand *kiddush HaShem* as a gift to a present God, who is ironically reflected in the very intelligence with which they discern the point at which they give their lives for God."

And yet there are times when God seems totally absent, when there are no observable traces of Godliness. In such a situation, how will we respond? Will the rational limits that we have set for ourselves still guide us? Would a God who resides in the world and is present in history permit our enemies to threaten us with mortal danger? The possible conclusions are only that I am a terrible sinner so I must deserve this, or maybe God isn't really there. But the faithful believer cannot accept either of these.

Such a situation of divine silence Shanks finds reflected in the Talmudic discussion between R. Akiba and Pappus

b. Yehudah, suggesting a third way to deal with God's absence and reacting to it. Pappus asks the rabbi whether he is not afraid of the authorities who have proscribed Torah study. Akiba responds with his famous parable of fish who are advised by the fox to escape the fishermen's nets by jumping onto dry land. To this suggestion, the fish reply: Do they really call you the cleverest of animals? You are not clever but foolish. If we are afraid in the element in which we live, how much more so in the element in which we would die (B.T. Berachot 61a). R. Akiba, like the friends of Daniel turned away by God, argues that in a time when God is distant, all that remains is to be oneself, to stay with oneself, in the element in which one lives, even when it seems less than rational.

Shanks finds a similar theme in the midrash that tells of Satan tempting Abraham on the way to the binding of his son. Despite the silence hovering over him on that three-day journey to Moriah, Abraham 'swims straight', loyal to himself. Satan callously intimates that Abraham deserves better. Abraham replies that he does not seek evidence of God in the world around him. All he can know is the rhythm and meter of his own holy trek. 'In my innocence, I will walk forward.'

"When the world is safe, God is everywhere" but when it is not, He must be found in the integrity of those who 'stick with' God. Shanks' suggestion, close to an educational one, is that we "learn to find God in the world around us when our situation enables us to, and in our hearts when we cannot."

One can question whether the example of R. Ishmael and the sages of Lydda well reflect divine Presence. The times are hardly a pinnacle of Jewish well-being! It is also easy to take issue with the thesis that rational discourse best represents times of divine Presence. But Shanks seems to move more than half-way from theology to educational vision. To an extent, she 'translates' Neher into an educational ideal. Like Daniel's companions, an educated Jew has learned to 'find' God everywhere 'when the world is safe', and is prepared to 'swim straight' through stormy waters when He is silent. At those times, a Jewish person has only his or her identity intact, believing and acting in the knowledge that autonomy is established and faith is somehow authenticated by the test of solitude. Character, it has been said, is what one is and what one does when one is alone – and no one is looking.

But the alone-ness is neither rugged individualism nor existential bravado. The educator reminds us that there is the community wherein identity is fashioned; that there is the text which testifies to divine speech. She reminds the reader of "self-evident divine Presence" that instructs its community how to survive in times of 'eclipse'. And there are one's teachers who set an example. Together they testify to an immovable identity. Or, as the theologian might say, together they are a *bat kol,* an echo of God's speech, remembered and anticipated.

In the educational ideal that flows from this conception, there is response, communal and individual, even when there is 'eclipse'. God's action or inaction is at times incomprehensible, but there is no early closure, no premature answers on what He is doing; only an active waiting. There is trust and hope.

Teaching for Faith; Walking in Innocence

In this vision, there is education for faith: speaking with children when God is 'near' and preparing them for when there might be hours of silence. For the identity of the child, if parents and teachers are wise and circumstances are not horrendous, is maximally built on a world that is safe, which, for the child, is one in which God is clearly present. The world, through the good offices of parents and teachers, is tentatively friendly, for it is a world in which God speaks, but it is not a rosy fairytale, for often, as every child knows and will later come to brood about, God may also be absent. Parents must also prepare the child for that world. It is one in which there is some safety, much anxiety, obstinate longing and courage. It is, I believe, the world that religious people in fact inhabit.

The question of whether the real world is the one of silence and chaos or of deep meaning can be asked because in an education of *hen-lo*, of 'yes' and 'no', there is, ideally, no fence-sitting. The community that socializes and the parents who rear may be said to represent the *Shekhinah*, the Divine Presence. But the terror is there too, for little children in the dark, and for all who have to decide, on dark days to come: Were my mentors and comforters telling the truth? Did they speak for God? Does God speak? Can He be trusted and relied upon?

The religious educator's entire enterprise is built upon the hope that the questioner will say *hen*, yes. Hopefully, he or she will remember, from moments experienced, decisions made, and actions and commitments 'seen through to the end', the reality of what he or she has learned to believe. Hopefully young people, asking that ultimate question, will see it as ludicrous to ask the God who has given them covenantal identity whether they can be relieved of it. But it is possible that they will cease to address Him because they know what His answer will be: that He will take them by the scruff of their necks, by the force of convention or habit, and make them listen even to His silence. Yet perhaps they will become fatigued by that silence; they may themselves become silent. This is the fear of every educator who dares to envision religiously-minded pupils.

Nevertheless, these questions will be asked, because a non-indoctrinating education will not socialize in a manner that inhibits the ability of the child to make decisions. After all, in an education which strives to present the truth, the facts – say, of the Holocaust – will not be denied. Terror cannot be read out of the curriculum, even if all this horror is presented with *halakhic* propriety and moral humility. Ultimately, each individual who merits to achieve a measure of spiritual maturity, may come to ask: But is it true? Can it obligate me? Shall I choose 'yes' or 'no'?

The educating community will urge the young person to loyalty; he or she is desperately needed there, in the community, to prevent the diminution of God's name in the world. He or she is witness to a trust that sees God even in concealment, and hope even in despair. His or her religious education has purposefully generated the inclination to choose to stay with it, to see God demanding it, to see the *hen-lo*, the 'yes' and the 'no' as inviting stubborn commitment, even unto martyrdom.

But where affirmative decisions are heroic, negative ones must also be within the realm of possibility. There must also be a place for silence. Otherwise even a religious affirmation to the community, to the library of Judaism and to what teachers stand for, is not sufficient – particularly after the Holocaust in which there was such horrendous aloneness. Otherwise it is not, in many senses, modern religiosity. For 'the child' is a factor in education, not only as a bundle of psychological stages but as a person who has been shown ways to walk forward and who ultimately must move, both in his or her own innocence and in search of it.

The silence of those who choose not to speak within the community of faith, may sound jarring indeed to religiously-minded educators. But perhaps human silence can also be saying something of religious significance. That question is likely to be a crucial one for secular as well as religious Jewish educators in this generation.

1. This essay is based largely on my "Theological Reflections on the Holocaust: Between Unity and Controversy", in Steven T. Katz (ed.), *The Impact of the Holocaust on Jewish Theology*, New York & London: New York University Press, 2005, pp. 161-174. Published here with permission.

2. Jacob Gladstein, quoted in Michael Berenbaum, *After Tragedy and Triumph: Modern Jewish Thought and the American Experience*, Cambridge UK: Cambridge University Press, 1990, p. 59

3. For discussion of the "sin of Zionism", see Menachem Friedman, "The Haredim and the Holocaust", *The Jerusalem Quarterly*, No.

53 (Winter 1990). In the religious world, the major exponent of the approach that it was sinful not to recognize the dawn of redemption in Eretz Yisrael is Rabbi Issachar Shlomo Teichthal, *Em Habanim Simehah*, Jerusalem: Pri Ha'aretz Institute, 5743. For an extensive discussion, see Eliezer Schweid, *Bein Hurban L'Yishhuah, (From Ruin to Salvation)*, Tel Aviv: Hakibbutz Hameuhad, 1994, Chap. 5. The ironical comment on National Socialists is R. Elhanan Bunim Wasserman's, himself, like Teichthal, a victim of the Holocaust. See his *Kovetz Maamarim*, Tel Aviv: published by his son, 5746, p. 119.

4. On the birth, the Shoah and the State of Israel in terms of an alleged Messianic process, see Uriel Tal, "The Land and the State of Israel in Israeli Religious Life", in *The Rabbinical Assembly Proceedings 1976*, New York: The Rabbinical Assembly, 1977, pp. 1-40. Menachem M. Kasher, *Israel Passover Haggadah*, New York: Shengold Publishers, 1983 (Seventh Edition) devotes an entire section to explaining the Messianic process underway on the basis of rabbinic texts.

5. Schweid, *Bein Hurban L'Yishuah*, especially Chap. 4.

6. Emil L. Fackenheim, *God's Presence in History*, New York: New York University Press 1970, especially pp. 33-30; 84-92.

7. Norman Lamm, "The Face of God: Thoughts on the Holocaust", in *Theological and Halakhic Reflections on the Holocaust*, Bemhard H. Rosenberg and Fred Heuman (eds.) Hoboken, N.J: Ktav Publishing House, Inc. 5752/1992, pp. 119-136. Citations are from pp. 127, 133.

8. Eliezer Berkovits, *Faith after the Holocaust*, New York: Ktav Publishing House, 1973. On R. Akiba, see pp. 80-85.

9. For example, J.B. Soloveitchik "Kol Dodi Dofek (The Voice of my Beloved Beckons)" in Soloveitchik, *Ish Ha'emunah (The Man of Faith)* Jerusalem: Mossad Harav Kook, 5731, (second printing), pp. 65-71.

10. Isaiah Leibowitz, *Yahadut, Am Yehudi V'Medinat Yisrael* (Judaism, the Jewish People, and the State of Israel), Jerusalem and Tel Aviv: Schocken, 5735/1975. See particularly, "Hinukh L'Mitzvot

(Education for the Commandments)" pp. 57-67; "Hamoreshet Hayehudit-Notzrit Hamishutefet (The Common Judeo-Christian Heritage)" pp. 327-333.

11. Note, for example, in much haredi literature of response, the main element is how to act properly and appropriately in the Holocaust situation. See Sarah Kaplan and Esther Ferbstein, *HaShoah beRei HaHalakhah: Iyun beShe'elot veTshuvot beHalakhah(Shotim) MeTekufat HaShoah – Yekhidat Limud (The Holocaust from the Perspective of Halakhah: Studies in Halakhic Responsa for the Period of the Holocaust – Study Unit)*, Jerusalem: Jerusalem College, 2009.

12. Fackenheim, *God's Presence in History*, pp. 20-21.

13. Eliezer Schweid, *Lihaggid Ki Yashar HaShem: Hazdakat Elohim b'Mahshevet Yisrael M'tikufat Hamikra V'ad Spinoza* (To Declare That God Is Upright: Theodicy in Jewish Thought), Bat Yam, Israel: Tag Publishers, 1994. For the discussion cited, pp. 9-12; *Maavak Ad Shahar (Wrestling Until Daybreak)*, Tel Aviv: Hakibbutz Hameuchad Publishing House, Inc., 1990. For discussion cited, see Chap. 7. It should be noted that Schweid does not rule out personal religious faith and experience. See *Liheyot Ben L'Am Hayehudi*, Tel Aviv: Akad 5752, where he elaborates on this. His discussion above revolves around the classic national theologies.

14. Richard L. Rubenstein, *After Auschwitz: Radical Theology and Contemporary Judaism*, Indianapolis: Bobbs-Merrill, 1966. See also, Rubenstein, "Jewish Theology and the Current World Situation", *Conservative Judaism*, Vol. 28, No. 4 (Summer 1974) for a statement of his pessimism.

15. See Joseph J. Schwab, "Translating Scholarship into Curriculum", in Seymour Fox and Geraldine Rosenfeld, *From Scholarship to the Classroom: Translating Jewish Tradition into Curriculum*, New York: Melton Research Center for Jewish Education, The Jewish Theological Seminary of America, 1977, pp. 1-30; Seymour Fox, "The Scholar, the Educator and the Curriculum of the Jewish School", in Ibid., pp. 104-114.

Michael Rosenak

16. On the misuse of psychological theories in education, see Joseph J. Schwab, "On the Corruption of Education by Psychology", *The School Review*, Vol. 78, No. 1 (Summer 1958), pp. 51-71.

17. Milton Rokeach, *The Open and Closed Mind; Investigations into the Nature of Belief System and Personality Systems*, New York: Basic Books, 1960, Chap. 3.

18. For the apparent incongruence here, see Shmot Rabbah 30:9 where God is portrayed as giving His laws to Israel, here interpreted as the self-same laws that He obeys, "unlike (kings of) flesh and blood, giving decrees to others and himself doing nothing..."

19. Ignatz Maybaum, *The Face of God After Auschwitz*, Amsterdam: Polak and van Gennep, 1965.

20. Emil L. Fackenheim, *God's Presence in History: Jewish Affirmations and Philosophical Reflections*, New York and London: New York University and University of London Press, 1970

21. Andre Neher, *The Exile of the Word: From the Silence of the Bible to the Silence of Auschwitz* (translated from the French by David Maisel), Philadelphia: The Jewish Publication Society, 5741/1981, pp. 199-207.

22. Ibid, p. 207

23. Elizabeth Shanks, "Dialogues on the Theme of Martyrdom", *Post-Modern Jewish Philosophy Network Journal*, Vol. 5, No. 1 (March 1996), Drew University, Madison, New Jersey, unpaginated.

V

The Concept of Jewish Peoplehood[1]

In this essay I wish to explore the concept of Jewish Peoplehood. Does "Peoplehood" describe something essential about Jewish existence? Does it point to some vision of Jewish life? And what has it to do with a theological conception of Judaism? How in general, then, is this notion useful? After all, have not the close-knit communities of "the people" virtually disappeared, the *amcha*, to whom the concept accorded a sense of identity and a focus of identification? How is it then that, despite the difficulties it raises, the notion of Peoplehood still seems so rich and promising and indeed is rising to the fore in the educational approaches of 21st century Jewish leadership?

Some possible reasons: Perhaps 'Peoplehood' remains helpful in enhancing Jewish life because the Peoplehood paradigm has the power to blur the great differences among Jews and still somehow hold them together, despite the variety of ways in which Jews discern themselves as Jews; despite the different degrees and kinds of their commitment; and despite the varied ways Jews see 'the other', both Jew and Gentile. Perhaps Peoplehood provides a prism through which we can acknowledge the differences between Jews without abandoning loyalty to them and self-identification with them. The concept of Peoplehood, then, may be helpful for us to become more fully aware of how these other Jews are different from ourselves even while we continue to search for commonalities among 'them', (whoever 'they' are) and ourselves, (whoever 'we' are). Obviously, if there were no such commonalities among Jews, 'Peoplehood' would lose all present-day meaning and all normative force, even if it remained useful in describing or imagining the Jewish past, nostalgically depicting 'life with the people'.

To come to grips with these questions and problems, we should examine some underlying issues in contemporary Jewish life and locate some concepts that may clarify matters.

Descriptive and Prescriptive Commonalities

The common ground we seek and hope to find among Jews, may be either descriptive or prescriptive or both. In the first, *descriptive,* mode, we ask what there is 'out there' that draws Jews together and how this Jewish 'togetherness' expresses itself in the public domain, open to research and analysis. In the second, *prescriptive,* mode we ask what do we see Jews doing, as visible manifestations of their diverse conceptions and assumptions about *what it means to be a Jew* and *what should be done* by Jews who perceive Judaism as significant and obligating?

Looking at matters through the first of these prisms, the descriptive one, we see Jews living in certain historical and existential situations that are clearly recognizable and seemingly inescapable and to which Jews ('naturally') respond as the given context suggests they do. For example on *Yom HaShoah* (Holocaust Memorial Day) we may expect them to have a heightened awareness of what we remember together and what bonds of kinship we share; what horrific animosities we have suffered and how we have responded to them. On the descriptive level, Jews continue to see themselves suffering from a mysterious bias directed against them and they remain aware of the untold aggression that was (and continues to be) directed against them, simply because they are Jews. These phenomena are still 'out there', in the media and on college campuses, as in the Purim memories of the wicked Haman, that hateful "adversary of the Jews". These memories and fears, as well as narratives of victory and vindication, still bring Jews together. The concept of Peoplehood can help place in context what Jews have endured and how they continue to respond – together.

However we cannot assume that such 'tribal' loyalties and bonds and responses will automatically and perennially protect the identity of Jews. We well know that there are increasing numbers of Jews who question the legitimacy of this deterministic 'situation' of (alleged) commonalities. In their view, presenting descriptive phenomena as though they were automatically prescriptive testifies to an ideological agenda of 'Jewish identity' that is parochial and manipulative. These people point out that if we are alarmed by the statistics of assimilation, then we too apparently believe that Jews, at least in today's world, do have the choice to get away from all that. Indeed, if Jewish culture and spirit are of negligible interest to them, *why not* get away? If there is nothing inherently valuable or interesting left as an existential ground for peoplehood, why stick with it? We shall return to this issue presently.

Visions and Commitments

As said, a second option in the search for commonalities is prescriptive. For the person seeking Jews and Judaism in the prescriptive domain, it matters not how gloomy the descriptive dimension of Jewish life is, and for that matter, how gloomy is human existence as such. They see themselves bound, as Jews, to a specific vision of life and humanity, bearing the imprint of some collective cultural or religious experience, intimating social order and fellowship, or holiness and compelling commitment. They seek to initiate their children into the life of a distinctive historical people or, they may say, a covenanted one. They feel that they are called to an individual and even a 'national' life of commandment, or, simply, and in a somewhat less theological vein, that Judaism demands that they be both decent and devoted.

As noted, this prescriptive view of what the Jews *ought to be*, rests on some descriptive foundations: after all, there do exist Jews, in significant numbers and in rich variety, who hold to such a prescriptive outlook and they can be described. But alas, research into such prescriptive Jews and types of Judaism, suggests that the contemporary forms of "prescriptive" Judaism do not seem to point to commonalities at all! After all, what is common in the life and beliefs of ultra-Orthodox Yeshiva persons and American Reform rabbis? What do dedicated Israeli generals, or for that matter, ultra-Orthodox Yeshiva oriented persons, share in the realm of culture and of spirit with Jewish feminists in Manhattan's Upper West Side? It would seem that the greater the prescriptive commitments of contemporary Jews, the more does prescription as such move engaged Jews away from commonality.

Covenant of Fate, Covenant of Destiny

The descriptive commonalities that do remain after the virtual collapse of spiritual communion and consensus among Jews have been described by Rabbi Joseph Soloveitchik as reflecting what he calls a "Covenant of Fate"; the prescriptive ones refer to what he calls a "Covenant of Destiny".[2] Note that Soloveitchik describes both in terms of a Jewish-divine relationship; they are both covenants. Both involve commanded action and both intimate significance.

I shall return to "the Covenant of Destiny", but here I am first concerned with the "Covenant of Fate" for it seems more amenable to description and more congenial to the search for commonalities. And despite the doubters, the covenant of fate is still really there for most Jews. It is what makes many Jews look for news about Israel first when they peruse the morning newspaper, and what makes them oddly uneasy at charges of undue Jewish influence in government and the arts. This all seems somewhat tragic but, as noted, Soloveitchik does not perceive the covenant of fate as 'tragic'. For him, it is part and parcel of the God-Israel relationship. Hence it demands a willingness to remain distinctive in attitude and action, and to foster unity in the face of persecution or vilification, and calls for effective response to them. And the demand Jews see as directed to them, to empathize with Jewish misfortune and to act in unison in the face of danger, is still commonly 'explained' by the simple statement that 'we are one people': in our common memories of sorrows endured, in our stubborn survival, in a perilous existence, ennobled by courageous response. Would another people have recreated its commonwealth after nineteen hundred years of exile, three years after the murder of one third of its members? Was this project of restoring the Jewish commonwealth not perceived by Jews as both commanded and redemptive, in whatever religious or secular ways they understood the concepts of commandment and redemption?

For this aspect of Jewish experience, this "Covenant of Fate" that describes an historical but also a contemporary reality, the term "Peoplehood", then, seems apt and useful. It seeks to promote Jewish self-identification without requiring shared religiosity, or a cultivation of national culture or large stores of national fervor, though all of these are cultural and existential options. On the religious plane, it does not mandate faith or even interest in God, or traditional commandments or institutional belonging. On the cultural plane it does not even require a common language; and it does not insist that all Jews come on *aliyah*, though many Israeli Jews might insist that the battles of the covenant of fate are fought on higher ground in Israel.

Is there another term that might serve us better than 'Peoplehood' to describe what draws Jews to one another? *Nationality* is certainly not appropriate today when the Jews are being reconstituted in Israel as a nation while Diaspora Jews remain by choice citizen-members of other nations. As for the term *religion*, while appropriate in the Diaspora for members of various denominations within which most engaged Diaspora Jews find their Jewish identities, it leaves out the secular Israeli almost in principle and many Jewish secular humanists world-wide.

So, Peoplehood still seems appropriate to describe the "fate" dimension of Jewish life. But if that were all that remained to engage our energies and to unite us, the ramifications would be deeply disturbing. If the most general aspect of being different is related to being acted upon, and of being suspect and strange, then we must ask: Do we have "a stake" in continued persecution and insecurity? What options are presented by an identity based on anti-semitism? Is 'fighting anti-semitism proudly' an ideal and perennial educational goal? Does it not, if viewed as the be-all and end-all of 'Peoplehood', contain the seeds of closed-mindedness, generated by a tragic awareness of living in an unfriendly world?

And turning the coin: Can Peoplehood be constructed on the denial of a fundamental tenet of Jewish faith and theology, namely, that in "times to come" (*b'acharit hayamim*) universal peace will be realized: that "nation shall not lift up sword against nation" and that the "kingdom of God" will be established and universally accepted?

These are of course, rhetorical questions. They are meant to suggest that we should not evade a search for a prescriptive formulation of Peoplehood that points to an educational ideal and community-wide vision. We wish to

187

Michael Rosenak

build a consciousness towards the idea that what unites us is more than what divides us, that beyond anti-semitism there is culture, however conceived and lived by. Yet given the ruptures in the fabric of Jewish life, the questions arise: How can this culture be presented and implemented in a manner that does not itself divide religious Jews from secular ones, Diaspora Jews from Israeli ones? How to break away from an obsession with consensus that all too often produces vacuous sloganeering instead of educated discourse?

One course of action that may 'move' Jewish Peoplehood and its implied vision of Jewish unity into the realm of some prescriptive Jewishness that is not banal, is to foster a community identity that leaves questions of belief, behavior and commitment open, yet important. The identity sought in this approach is one that demonstrates a readiness to be informed by the past but leaving the present and the future open, 'even' to traditional paradigms. This proposed course of action suggests that we explore the past without prejudice, willing to learn from it, studying the Great Jewish Books in order to discover and clarify previous models of Jewish distinctiveness. Then, whether through cursory acquaintance with 'the Jewish bookcase', or profound study of it, we may discover that Jewish identity, and the uniqueness of the Jews as a group, have taken on many forms: tribal and monarchistic, a rabbinic culture of Torah, a dispersed people settled around Jewish religious law, mystic communities and 'learning' ones, pioneering kibbutzim and Hebrew creativity. On the basis of the dynamics of Jewish history and culture as we find them in 'the Jewish bookcase', we are likely to find today's inner struggles for more – or less – change not so uncomfortable, and not so threatening in our search for commonalities. Why shouldn't Jewish distinctiveness be characterized, among other things, by disagreement and diversity? Yet, even the important modern, 'prescriptive', development of Jewish learning does not clearly move Peoplehood onto center stage. After all, most of those standing before the Jewish bookshelf were not so far removed from it to begin with!

So, objections remain. Why be responsible or committed? Why stand stubbornly behind a notion of Peoplehood that is so obviously problematic? Isn't the "Covenant of Fate" all that actually remains, at least for most Jews, with its 'curriculum' of survival, to which it is difficult to educate wholeheartedly in a free society? Who can blame young people who walk away from all that, and who find flight from Jewish identity not only do-able, but liberating as well?

(Not So) Hidden Assumptions

So why is there an adherence to a formula of "Jewish unity" based upon a "Covenant of Fate"? It seems to me that Jewish leaders who are so 'taken' with the concept of Peoplehood are consciously or unconsciously basing themselves on specific assumptions as to what is 'out there', and hence, a certain (gloomy) view of what can be salvaged. Yet these assumptions, if they are indeed central to the thinking of contemporary Jews, may turn out to be unduly narrow, limiting our ability to think of alternative solutions to the sundry problems of Jewish continuity – and the possibilities inherent in them. What are these assumptions?

Assumption One: Unless 'something is done' to revitalize the Jewish people, the demise of the Jews as an historic community is virtually certain, even if some ultra-Orthodox groups will remain as a sectarian remnant. (Strangely, those who profess not to fear for their survival, the Haredim, appear in this model to be part of the problem when in fact they present a certain kind of solution, no matter how unpalatable to some.)

Assumption Two: While Jewish civilization has been predominantly religious, attempts to make religious faith and practice the foundations for Jewish existence in our time is unrealistic and intellectually unacceptable. We all, Jews and non-Jews, live in a secular, pluralistic world, increasingly globalized and "post-modern".

Assumption Three: While we are loving children of the Enlightenment, it must be admitted that all interesting or important things that have happened to Jews since the dawn of Enlightenment have been ultimately corrosive and have contributed to the demise of tradition and Jewish community.

Each of these assumptions exposes different problems to view and each leads to particular types of action, often positive. The first assumption requires drawing wider circles of Jews into activities that will create identification and positive Jewish experience. A notable example of solving the problem of the disappearance of the Jews is in "Israel experiences" and, at the other end of the continuum, Holocaust curricula. The second and third assumptions have led policy makers in the direction of Zionism, Jewish Community Centers, camping (for all age groups and for families) and intellectually-oriented educational programs for Jewish leadership These assumptions also suggest expanding on programs and university studies dealing with the relationship between Jews and modernity, and encouraging frameworks for Jewish experience.

While these three assumptions have proven their value in the policies and programs they have fostered, they are not the only ones by which to understand the Jewish situation. Let us take a second look at them:

(a) The Jews are disappearing; they are a threatened species.

The fear that the Jews are about to vanish from the face of the earth is not new and has, at least from the days of the Destruction of the Second Commonwealth and the fall of Massada and Betar, always been with us. Articulations of this fear are well documented by Simon Rawidowicz.[3] In his classic article: "Israel: The Ever Dying People" he argues that this mindset of "being the last ones" has accompanied Jews from time immemorial. For Rawidowicz, the flip side of this consciousness of "the ever dying people" is *the never-dying people.* In this context we may note one of the amazing facts to emerge from research on post-World War II European Jewish survivors: In the years after the Shoah, the *she'arit hapleta,* Jews in displaced persons camps, had one of the highest group birth rates in the world.[4] This chapter of post-Holocaust history may surely stand alongside the establishment of Israel, a mere three years after the Shoah! Both events take place without a doubt within the parameters of the "Covenant of Fate". Both are readily conceptualized by way of 'Peoplehood'. But the energies they generated seem to point beyond that.

191

Michael Rosenak

(b) Religion can no longer serve as a basis for Jewish life; the People rather than God must be placed at the center of Jewish consciousness."

Is this really so? What is the role of religion in maintaining the Jews, in the past and at present? What do we know about it? It can be argued that the world has not become more irreligious at all! True, there has been an increase of secular consciousness, even to an extent among Jewish and other fundamentalists and this consciousness gives rise to new religious thinking. The fact is that many scholars who research religion have indeed moved away from it and have tended to project their (secular) ideologies onto the subjects of their inquiries. Religion, then, may have changed, even radically, but that was in large measure to maintain its relevance!

(c) Ever since the Enlightenment, Jews have been acted upon by the outside world and its enlightened philosophies in variegated ways, all of which have impacted negatively on Jewish identity, faith and culture. Jews, like almost all others, have become modern, to the detriment of the tradition that kept Jewish civilization alive and made it the instrument of salvation for the Jews.[5]

Yet we may ask: Is that all that has happened? Would there have been such significant and fascinating Jewish movements as Modern Orthodoxy and post-modern Reform, Zionism, or 'Jewish Studies', without the Enlightenment? Would there have been significant quasi-prophetic figures like Kafka, traditionalist innovators such as Eliezer Berkovits, political leaders like Ben Gurion, scholars like Gershom Sholem, sage mystics like Rabbi Avraham Hacohen Kook, creative theologians like Franz Rosenzweig and Emmanuel Levinas? Would all, like ultra-Orthodox Jews, wish to live without the insights, possibilities and challenges that characterize their lives as modern?

Certainly, the way we cut the cake makes a difference in the ways we discuss 'Peoplehood' issues. For example: Shall we provide more funding and channel energies in educating the committed, or should we foster outreach? To cite British Chief Rabbi Jonathan Sachs[6]: Must we tell the sparsely committed and virtually unconnected that without them the Jews will vanish? Or, that they are likely to miss out on the adventure of the Jewish future?

Two Ways of Cutting the Cake

One of my teachers, the late Professor Nathan Rotenstreich of the Hebrew University, once presented me with two ways of conceptualizing and reading modern Jewish history, and two ways of teaching it.

Way One: "The Jewish Problem" and the Jewish Reaction:

In the first of the two readings of history, Jews are acted upon by others and then react in turn. One can, said Rotenstreich, 'open' the annals of modernity with the French Revolution, moving then to the rise of the nation-state with its demand for loyalty, addressed to all citizens. This will bring us to the Emancipation, the apparent acceptance of Jews as equal citizens, and the subsequent growth of anti-semitism. In this particular Jewish history syllabus, attention would be paid to European socialist movements and to their Jewish counterparts, the Bund and then to socialist Zionism. There would be a study of European nationalism and of Jewish nationalism as a response, especially to those national movements that depicted the Jews as 'a problem'. This course in modern Jewish history would suggest seeing the Holocaust as proof that Jewish 'normalization' was an illusion, vindicating the auto-emancipation of the Jews through political Zionism. Paradoxically, in the lands of liberalism there would also be a fear for Jewish survival despite the embrace of normalizing societies of freedom. Here Jewish experience would not generally include being acted upon in a negative fashion but, rather, of being granted rights, and, hence, of 'enjoying' the option to assimilate. Responses such as "never again" and the creation of the State of Israel out of the ashes of the Holocaust are the ground on which Jews build institutions and movements designed to counter the forces of cultural assimilation.

Way Two: Jewish Cultural Distinctiveness and Ingenuity:

Rotenstreich's second way of reading modern Jewish history also comes replete with a syllabus of its own. Here the emphasis is on internal experience and self-expression. The focus is on cultural initiatives that are indelibly Jewish, and on the distinctive qualities of Jewish culture. In this second scheme, we begin modern Jewish history with the messianic movement of Shabbtai Zvi, and trace the development of the Hasidic and even the Reform movements as post-Sabbatean developments. Hasidim would be studied, not only for its innovative spiritual modes and messages, but also in the context of the threat it posed to the scholarly and *halakhically* normative modes of traditional rabbinic leadership. The ensuing polemic would also be examined through non-Hasidic teachings as these developed within the Lithuanian '*Yeshiva* world', with its study of Talmudic literature, its adherence to ever more strict *halakhic* standards, and its moral fervor as found in the "Mussar" movement.[7] Units of study would be devoted to the polemics surrounding the issue of modernity which undermined the Lithuanian and Hasidic worlds alike.

Students would learn about radically traditional rabbis who denounced everything new as forbidden by the Torah,[8] and would explore ultra-Reform and secular faiths as well as new forms of Jewish life such as the kibbutz, and modern expressions in Yiddish and Hebrew literature and Jewish music. The debate in modern Jewry about 'religion' and tradition will be seen to have engendered Jewish 'movements' that fought over the essence of Judaism. In this syllabus too, anti-semitism is present as an issue but it appears as an ideological challenge, or a theological one. As for Zionism, it is, in this scheme of things, more about such cultural figures as Ahad Ha-am and Brenner and Rabbi A.I. Kook,[9] first Chief Rabbi of modern Palestine, than about politically-oriented persons like Theodore Herzl and Max Nordau, for what stands at the center of its concerns is not the 'problem of the Jews' but 'the problem of Judaism'.

A subsequent question: How should one read the Holocaust? Were the atrocities perpetrated the birth pangs

Michael Rosenak

of the Messiah or a harbinger of 'the death of God' that would fundamentally change Judaism? The rise of Israel too could be variously interpreted: Was it the 'beginning of our redemption' or an opportunity for self-redemption from the economic, social and religious forms and the varied deformities of exilic life?

What would "Jewish Peoplehood" signify in each approach?

In terms of Soloveitchik's "covenants", Rotenstreich can be seen to be asking whether modern Jewish history is mainly about "fate" or about "destiny". Paradoxically, if we are an historical entity only by virtue of what was done to us, whether through force, persuasion or influence, then the "Covenant of Fate" clearly marks the limits of Jewish Peoplehood. One need not be a certain type of Jew nor is it necessary to have a particular engagement with "Covenant of Destiny" in order to feel a sense of belonging to the Jews and to act upon it, for example, through political Zionism. Israelis and Diaspora Jews, religious and secular, can work together in anti-defamation ventures, can rejoice together at victories and cry together in defeat. They can be stubbornly loyal to their small and harried people, and celebrate their endurance. They may even, like Soloveitchik, view the establishment of Israel, coming in the wake of the Holocaust, as a singular achievement, imposed by God, whose covenant demands enduring fate, but also withstanding it. Both are manifestations of Jewish peoplehood. Yet, as already noted, Peoplehood that is all "Covenant of Fate" is problematic; educationally, culturally – and theologically.

In the proactive and positive understanding of Jewish Peoplehood, we anticipate a time when the hatred of others, and their foreboding other-ness, will no longer set *our* agenda for self-understanding, response or responsibility.

Jews and their "Peoplehood" – and Beyond That

The relationship of Jews to their sense of being one people, to the totality of their complex identities, is a puzzling one, and to the nations of the world, often exasperating. It can, however, be clarified by way of various historical perspectives. Let us briefly explore the issue on the basis of some early records of Jewish self-awareness, by way of several biblical narratives.

When leaving Egypt where they had become a people, at least in Pharoah's eyes (compare Exodus 1:7 and 1:9), the Israelites remembered the cucumbers they had eaten there and some wished to return on their account to Egypt (Numbers 11:5), as though being an enslaved or a free people was of minor matter, less momentous than cucumbers.

Later, when settled in their land under the rule of Judges, they wanted a king like the other nations, ignoring the pleas of leaders like Gideon (Judges 8:22-23) and Samuel (I Samuel 8) to forego mortal kings, for "God will rule over you".

When the monarchy split into two, after a rather brief unified 'national' existence, the kings and princes of the time hardly created a feeling of peoplehood, nor did they feel bound by any such notion. The two 'countries' were frequently at war with each other, and made alliances with foreign powers to better defeat the 'other' (Israelite or Judean) kingdom.

We have no evidence that the destruction of the Northern Kingdom in 719 B.C.E left the citizens of the southern kingdom of Judea in deep mourning. The historian Heinrich Graetz states unequivocally what he saw as the prophetic message of that time. "So estranged was that kingdom from those who recorded the memorials of the Israelitish nation, that they devoted but few words to its decline." As for the destruction itself, as Graetz would have it, "…the diseased limb that had infected the entire body of the nation, was cut off and rendered harmless."[10] And while the destruction of Judea itself in 586 B.C.E., together with Solomon's Temple, was an occasion for liturgies and lamentations, it too was, inexplicably, not perceived as 'the end'. After all, it had all been foretold by the prophets who spoke in God's name. These prophets, clearly men of prescription, were unique *national* figures, belonging to Israel and Judea together. They towered over kings and were unimpressed by the twin kingdoms that were like unto all the nations in their corruption and unique only in their 'faithlessness' to the God who had covenanted them to Himself. They were the spokespersons of destiny and they had a working concept of Peoplehood, of a people that was Judea and Israel alike. How many now remember that Elijah and Amos and Hosea were 'northerners', and that Isaiah, who prophesized in the name of *Kadosh Yisrael*, the Holy One of Israel, was a Judean?

The thoughtful Judean of the time probably 'knew' that there was a reason for the destruction and the suffering. And the prophets constantly asserted what the authors of the books of Kings and earlier biblical books had previously insisted: that the only important "national" issue for both kingdoms was whether they and their 'kings' would be loyal to their covenant with God, recognizing Him as their king. Would they be "wholehearted" with Him? This covenant was eternal. So when it was all over with these kingdoms, it wasn't all over after all. And since the destruction was not the end of the matter, the prophets, after their threats had been verified, became comforters. Did not even Jeremiah, most melancholy of Judea's prophets, promise in the name of God, that His people would yet "buy houses and fields and vineyards in this land"[11]?

But the people of that time, and commentators on the annals of our early history to this day, found other signs of continued life of "the ever dying" people as well. To give an astounding example: The Book of II Kings ends with a description of the courteous manner with which the Babylonian king, Evil-Marduk, treated the prisoner king, Yehoyachin, last remaining king of Judaea. Scripture relates that he took him out of prison, "spoke kindly to him," had him eat at his table and gave him an allowance. Why, after the total destruction of Judea and Jerusalem, end the Book of Kings with such a jarring anti-climax, with the good manners of a pagan king to the hapless representative of the Davidic line, of a far and distant Jewish glory? It seems a pathetic scene. Yet note how one popular twentieth century English commentator on II Kings (25:28-30) views the situation:

> The Book of Kings in its last four verses *concludes on a bright note*. The last surviving sovereign of Judah is set free from the rigours of his Babylonian prison. He is shown honor, kindness and good will. In this early period of the captivity, the historian detects an incident which is a hopeful augury for the future of his people, *a sign of the end of the exile and the restoration of the Davidic monarchy* (all italics mine – MR).[12]

Truly, however much it seems to be over, the reader of the Bible knows that it isn't.

This way of seeing matters is not idiosyncratic in Jewish history. Note that some time after the return of a Judean remnant from Babylonia, Ezra, a leader of the fledgling community of Jerusalem, initiates a fierce polemic after his arrival from Babylon. He demands that the foreign ("Samaritan") wives be expelled. He foresees that these women will corrupt the Judeans ('Jews') inducing them to idolatrous practices (Ezra 9). It has been argued that the Book of Ruth was written in that same period. If so, it seems clear that there were others who disagreed with Ezra, who argued, through the prism of an (even then) ancient tale, that even a daughter of the despised Moabite nation, like Ruth in the days of the Judges, could become a mother of royalty and forebear of the Messiah. Should such a devoted woman, whose archetypical story became a little biblical book of its own, be expelled? And what is to be said for a culture that argues about such matters when all seems to be over?

When scholars like Rawidowicz, declare that the Jews will never cease, they claim to be basing themselves on evidence, for they are scholars. However, like all scholars, they work on certain assumptions that underlie their scholarship. When they make statements of hope and faith, are they whistling in the dark, or perhaps pointing to intimations of the "covenant of destiny" that is 'out there', waiting to be examined, to be used?

Whistling in the Dark?

The work of Jewish community leaders in Israel and the Diaspora toward goals which seem fantastical and even imaginary, though they are characteristically termed "visions", is evidence of a kind for the axioms of the Jewish tradition that are reflected in the biblical passages cited above. But what kind of evidence is it? What now counts as evidence for the working assumptions of post-Holocaust Jews that 'it isn't the end and it won't be'?

This question arose in my mind during a learning session some forty years ago at Jerusalem's Institute for Youth Leaders from Abroad, an educational institution of the World Zionist Organization generally referred to, simply and endearingly, as "the Machon". On the occasion I have in mind, the Machon was being addressed by Professor Marshall Sklare, the noted mid-twentieth century American Jewish sociologist. Sklare brought many talents to his work, and great honesty. As early as 1964 he had warned his readers in an article in *Commentary*[13] that the statistics presented by alleged experts on intermarriage in the United

States were vastly misleading. American Jews would inevitably have to decide whether they wished simply to be members of American society or to maintain their own identities as somewhat, and significantly, different; a decision that he considered fateful for Jewish survival in America. In his talk at the Machon, he touched on diverse signposts of decline: in demography, in what he called the decline of Jewish 'cultural compulsions', that is, in the inability of Jews to connect Jewish artifacts and experiences with others undergone and experienced. Looking around the classroom with the practiced eye of a teacher, I saw that all our young 'machon-nikim', Jewish leaders to be, were crestfallen. Finally one took the initiative: "But Professor Sklare, everything you say points to the demise of the Jewish people." Sklare somberly admitted this to be so. "But then," said the unhappy machon-nik, "there is no future for us." Sklare became vehement. "God forbid." "But on the basis of what you have taught us..." continued the young madrich. Sklare cut him off: "All I said, I said as a sociologist. What I am telling you now, namely that the future of the Jews is assured, I say as a believing Jew." The Orthodox youth leaders in the audience were elated, the Hashomer Hatzair leaders wondered what he meant by 'belief' and whether he was a fundamentalist in disguise, and the Conservative Sklare – smiled.

All of us have seen and been touched by much evidence of the sometimes absurd manifestations of Jewish vitality. And yet, because we often espouse a "Covenant of Fate" conception of Jewish Peoplehood, for the reasons already discussed, we may sometimes miss them. Among these manifestations are the music of Shlomo Carlebach and his many associates and disciples, now sung enthusiastically by thousands in synagogues of all kinds; the renaissance of Jewish learning and the revolution in Torah study among women; the rebirth of the Hebrew language and the flowering of Hebrew literature; the great increase in Jews who wear *kipot* of various kinds[14] in public, certainly on the streets of Israel and North America; and the abundance of 'Israel experiences' and their continued growth.

From whence the energies, the stamina and the hope? I shall return to this question below. But first, I shall speak briefly of what counts as evidence for the future of the Jews through the prism of a story told to me by a Polish-born friend, a Holocaust survivor, a rational and unsentimental man. My friend, having escaped from the Warsaw Ghetto, went on to become a senior Jewish educator in the United States, and eventually came on *aliyah*, to Jerusalem and the Hebrew University. On his return from a visit to his native Poland, he had a strange and moving experience. Arriving at the Warsaw airport for the return trip to Tel Aviv, he discovered that his flight was slightly delayed. Some passengers, he saw, were visibly delighted at the delay for it gave them time to organize a *minyan*[15] to recite the afternoon prayer, to *"daven minchah"'* which they would otherwise have had to do, in some discomfort, on the plane. A *minyan* of some tens of Jews was rapidly convened and the 'davening' commenced. My friend, though not particularly pious, found himself joining the worshippers. Some days later, in Jerusalem, I found him ironic yet astounded. "Do you know what this means?" declared my soft-spoken friend. I replied, "I suppose some of these people thought they were in New York or London or Tel Aviv." He was enthused. "All right," he admitted. "But even that is amazing! Think for a moment. Once there were three million Jews there and *then* it could never have happened. Unthinkable, for Jews to make a *minyan*, to perform a collective Jewish act in a public place in Poland! So why is that now possible?" His voice rose in excitement. "Only one reason! The existence of the State of Israel! We [Jews] now have a state! So we can pray together right in front of the Poles!"

This was certainly a 'Peoplehood' experience, that seemingly took place within the confines of "fate"! Three million Polish Jews had perished and, in some absurd sense that the authors of II Kings and some commentators on it might have understood, *we had overcome* – by praying in public in a Polish airport. Absurd – because Poland remained a monstrous cemetery and there was no bringing these millions back to life; as absurd as seeing a harbinger of Redemption in the pathetic Yehoyahin being seated at the king's table and receiving a monthly allowance.

But the essential root of the story did not come up in our conversation which was, indeed, about 'Peoplehood' and the Covenant of Fate. For what led to this experience, and without which it couldn't have happened, was actually about destiny, namely, that these Jews *had to daven minchah*. They belonged to that sector of Jewry that considered itself bound to an idiosyncratic action, behind which stood God's commandment to be a holy people.

It is unlikely that most of the 'daveners' in question particularly reflect on that most of the time, and some of them may not know how to do that; in a sense, the paucity of their systematic reflection was part of the strength of their behavior. But that "Covenant of Destiny" was nevertheless the reason for which they had been educated to pray, by teachers and parents, those who were believed to understand about the covenant of destiny. They were the teachers who had taught the parents of the contemporary *daveners* to teach their children, now standing at the airport, to pray. That 'explained' several tens of Jews standing and swaying at the Warsaw airport. These Jews lacked some of the concepts and conceptions through which my friend thought, even as he lacked some of theirs. So, they probably didn't much think of having 'overcome'; rather, they were pre-occupied with the thought that it was "time for *minchah*". And the fact remained that the excitement of my friend and my own stopped short of touching on the "Covenant of Destiny", what it meant for those Jews to "do" Judaism and what it meant for my friend to be the kind of Jew that he was: more secular than they, but completely engaged in the mystery of Jewish existence. It was, after all, this destiny and this experience of Jewish norms dwelling within transcendence that lay behind the whole story, and made the event possible to begin with.

The Covenant of Destiny as reflecting Peoplehood gives rise to rich questions, but these can be explosive. For example: When these Jews recited the *Ashrei* prayer that opens the *minchah* service, what were they doing? How, in post-Holocaust Poland, could they repeat the verses of the *Ashrei*, "God is good to all and His tender mercies are upon all His creatures" and "God is righteous in all His deeds and gracious in all His works"? The *daveners* may consider the articulation of these questions as betraying the status of the questioner as an outsider, in which case the *minyan* at the airport, a prescriptive act, may once again demonstrate how commitment may unravel Peoplehood. But there is another possibility: that such questions draw even those who don't regularly pray into the realm of the "Covenant of Destiny" that prayer signifies. For here are questions raised for everyone viewing that airport scene: what are the meanings behind Jewish peoplehood that are accessible to us? What are the meanings that engendered Jewish feminism, more philosophy of Judaism, more Jewish schools, more Jewish study vigils throughout the night of Shavuot, and more 'Israel experiences' for Jewish youth? What does the evidence say?

Some years ago, a young man from the former Soviet Union applied to a prestigious teacher training institute in Jerusalem, wishing to spend two years of study, to be a fellow at that Institute. I interviewed him, as a faculty member of the Institute, at a camp site not far from Moscow, formerly belonging to the Young Communist League. This site was hosting a ten-day seminar in Judaism and Jewish leadership and I had been invited to teach within this framework. The young man, after a long journey by rail, came into the seminar camp hesitatingly, as though not trusting his eyes, not certain he was in the right place. Standing at the gate to the complex, he asked a young participant: "Is this the place? Is this the seminar for studying Judaism?" He was happily re-assured; he had come to the right place. As he came into the grounds of the seminar center, my mind turned from the textual lesson I was preparing, for I could not help but think how many new things, amazing things, were going on around me: a young man who walks in from nowhere in search of Jewish study *that is actually available;* the pilgrim's question whether he is embarked on the right road; the tiring trip from Odessa to the hinterland of Moscow that leads to *Yerushalayim Habenuyah,* to a rebuilt Jerusalem. Does that count as evidence?

Laying the Cards on the Table

I have attempted to show how the concept of Peoplehood is readily applied to the 'fate' aspect of Jewish existence, one that makes no specific cultural, religious or national demands. But I have pointed out that this will only be the case as long as our relationships with the nations of the world remain problematic. Today, as noted, many young Jews believe that they can simply walk away from it all. This may be an illusion; it may be true that in most circumstances Jews really have 'no choice', but if that is shown to be the case, it would not, or should not, evoke elation. For everlasting enmity can only strengthen young people's suspicions that 'they (the others who hate us) might be right'.

In the "Covenant of Destiny", Peoplehood enjoys a richer content, yet is less visible and persuasive, for in our present situation, concepts of 'destiny' are often divisive. At times they are even imbued with the consciousness of 'a righteous remnant' which alienates most Jews and makes meaningful uses of 'Peoplehood' unattainable. How then to make 'Peoplehood' a significant platform for living Jewish lives and for planning the Jewish future?

Rotenstreich partially alleviates our problem. While the Jews as an acted-upon group look like a people (since they are called upon to react collectively to the fate of being acted upon), this is not necessarily a long term scenario. For the ultimate goal of the actors is to effectively eradicate the Jews or absorb them, in each case 'saving' them from their fate as a living and distinctive community. And in an 'open society', the absorption of the Jews into the general culture and society is uniquely attractive. For in such an open society Jews may expect to be publicly and festively applauded for their contributions to the general culture and to its religious civilization. Rotenstreich is arguing that Jewish Peoplehood should be moved to the sphere of "destiny"; he suggests that it may be possible to speak persuasively of 'Jewish Peoplehood' in terms of the different ways in which modern Jews are engaged in conversation, and dispute, about the different ways they live their Jewish lives.

But that outcome, of variegated shapes and forms of Jewish life, is not inevitable. Despite the impressive communities and individuals who are making Judaism more interesting than it has been for a long time, there may simply not be enough Jews engaged in these conversations; and Judaism, even when innovative and spiritual, may seem jarring against the backdrop of the liberal societies in which almost all Jews now live.

Moreover, making Jewish Peoplehood an outcome of the covenant of destiny requires that those who think most of destiny, who have committed themselves to it and who live by one of its several visions, cultivate a largeness of spirit to go with their certainties, and reach for pluralism and open-mindedness, nurtured by a love of the Jewish people. But here we encounter difficulties that require careful thought.

Eliezer Goldman, the late Israeli thinker, has pithily pointed to the core of the dilemmas with which we are dealing.[16] He was an active participant in the historic Jerusalem Ideological Conference convened by David Ben Gurion in August 1957, in which the leading thinkers, statesmen and leaders of mid-century Jewry were invited to discuss the central issues of the day. Their task was to articulate diverse positions on the continuum of Jewish existence, to make recommendations about the Jewish situation, to discuss the place of religion and Zionism in present-day Jewish life and to express their views on the effect of Israel on Jewish communities and Jewish consciousness.

Goldman, an analytic philosopher, commented bitingly on a thesis proposed by several other participants that had urged strengthening the consciousness of Peoplehood as a primary educational goal. Goldman insisted that the historical facts of Jewish existence, 'the Jewish heritage' as described by historians and other scholars, were, by their very nature, non-obligatory. They were, after all, only "descriptive". Hence, said Goldman:

> There is no question here concerning the obligation towards the cultural heritage [i.e., there is no such obligation]. The heritage is a historical channel through which the sentiment of obligation, among other things, reaches us [though they come from outside the "heritage"]. The heritage [is the "channel" that bring into view] …obligations to God and to man. It [the cultural heritage] is in itself not the object of obligation. Even the people as an historical entity are not the object of obligations, [though the heritage and the People make these obligations accessible].[17]

Goldman then suggests two roads toward a significant Jewish life for our times. One is in line with Rotenstreich's experience of being acted upon. On this level, the question of national belonging is not one that is subject to the decision of the will but is determined by objective causes: persecution, economic separations, common identifying characteristics, etc. As a result of these causes, Goldman maintains, "no man can escape his Jewishness" and the existence of a "national sentiment can be taken for granted… and can be made the basis for further development."[18] This is the realm of "fate" as we have discussed it.

But there is a second way. It is "to attempt to extract from the Jewish heritage those values that we acknowledge as obligatory and then try to bend our national attitude towards them. National life then becomes an attempt to embody these values and the obligations which eventually flow from the values."[19]

In the address being cited here, Goldman makes four points. First, that national belonging can arise from objective causes, what we have called "fate".[20] Second, he is saying that, in themselves, descriptions of Jewish life, of historical developments and even of the former experience of 'Jewish Peoplehood', make no claims for allegiance to the data they are describing. Why indeed should past facts, however enthusiastically researched, and even descriptions of past beliefs, however moving, have the power to coerce to normative allegiance? (Yet we should recognize that many enter descriptive research into Jewish fields of study because they themselves are prescriptively endowed, and think, correctly or incorrectly, that they will infect others with their enthusiasms.) Third, loyalty to the Jewish people or for that matter to any social or institutional framework arises out of that institution's clear usefulness, its demonstrated power to serve human needs, and, often even the need for a sense of historical continuity *for those who seek it.* Fourth, that only the values we see as obligatory can protect and foster what we are calling Jewish Peoplehood, and then only if we experience these values as embedded in the life of our people, of its history and its faith. The educational upshot is that these values must be transmitted to us through the channels of our national culture. Once we have received these values through the channels of our culture, the values must 're-make' the nation and the culture in their own image. These values must interpret 'and bend' the facts of peoplehood to its transcendent or, if you will, its commanded, life.

Goldman's perspective is an Orthodox one: for him 'the People' exist for the sake of the "covenant of Judaism" that makes our collective lives an occasion of destiny. Hence he can say that "there are Jews such as myself, who do not recognize the right of any Jew to free himself from the yoke of any mitzvah."[21] True, Goldman declares that he feels a sense of deep kinship with Jews who do not see Jewish peoplehood as inherently 'bringing to them' a demand that they observe the laws of the Torah, but this sense of kinship is itself derived and nourished from Jewish norms and values: "If such Jews [as myself] encourage others who are far from Judaism to cultivate what is close to their hearts and regard them as their brothers, it is not because we recognize their right to free themselves [from the mitzvot] but because we understand the concept of *'Am Yisrael'* as including those who do not observe the norm."[22]

In short: it is the prescriptive Halakhah that determines the value of Jewish peoplehood; non-observant Jews are a part of the Jewish people because that is how 'we' (i.e., the halakhic Jews) understand the norm of fraternity with *Am Yisrael*, namely as a requirement of the Halakhah itself.

As discussed in the Introduction, Martin Buber examined the issue from a non-Orthodox perspective. His national-religious thesis is that the Jewish people underwent a unique occurrence in human history. "Only in one instance do [religion and nation] coincide. Israel receives its decisive experience *as a people;* it is not the prophet alone but the community as such that is involved."[23] Jews became a community of faith *and* a nation at one and the same time.

Zionism in its national-political aspects, is at its best an attempt to provide a ground for the Jews to be themselves.

In its social, cultural and spiritual aspects, Zionism ideally seeks to 'hear' what is now being 'said' to Jews: that Judaism is not simply a religion (of 'religious experience') undergone by individual believers, nor is it a nation (of memories and as the aspirations of a historical collective). Israel's task is "to assume the yoke of the kingdom of God". However the first, political, dimension should not be cast aside.

> Since this [the life of dialogical faith] can be accomplished only in the rounded life of a community, we must reassemble, we must again gain roots in the soil, we must govern ourselves. But these are mere *pre-requisites!* Only when the community recognizes and realizes them as such in its own life, will they serve as the cornerstones of its salvation.[24]

Buber is not pleading for a 'return to tradition' or for observance of the commandments. Indeed, he himself was not traditional and did not observe the traditional commandments. For him, "revelation" is a product of dialogue, a conversation between friends and fellows, an encounter with a Presence that energizes even as it makes ever-new demands of people. Buber cannot share Goldman's (to him) doctrinaire view of what is prescriptive in Jewish life. He will insist that we never know what God is demanding until we are open to the religious experience of this moment, rooted in 'the life of the nation'.

Yet he will agree with Goldman that Peoplehood and its culture are requirements of the uniquely Jewish spiritual life, and that Peoplehood may not be confused with that life. Should the 'yoke of Heaven' be forgotten or neglected, and all that remains is 'the people'; or, alternately, if there is no more than Jewish religious tradition, a 'faith' that makes do without existential ties to the Jewish people, the Jews are doomed, at best, to a sterile existence:

> We cannot substitute a technical association of nation and religion for this original marriage, without incurring barrenness.[25]

The thesis I have been presenting, that is indebted to Goldman and Buber, is that 'Peoplehood' is a meaningful and operative concept. But Peoplehood alone, as a concept that can point to the need to solve Jewish problems, and that can build on experience of unity in the midst of diversity, will become archaic. Without the heady experience of not being excluded and dehumanized, of not having to consider particular 'Jewish problems' as their problems, Peoplehood would become redundant as Jews become fully absorbed into non-Jewish societies. Peoplehood requires not the descriptive conception (of 'Peoplehood') but the intent of Jews to find ultimate meaning in the prescriptions that 'arise out' of Jewish life, and that are actually lived out by the Jewish people in a framework of valuative obligation. Then (or rather, now) Sklare's warning that Jews need to retain cultural distinctiveness, even in the open societies in which they live, constitutes a central challenge. Without moving towards a destiny that has common elements, however variegated, everything about 'Jewish Peoplehood' will come to depend on "fate". This scenario may at times be heroic but it is profoundly cheerless.

In Summation

The concept of Peoplehood, as we have seen, is a foundation stone of deliberations regarding a viable, vital and creative Jewish life. It allows the blurring of distinctions when blurring is called for by the common tasks at hand and when there is a need to organize collective energies for response to problems, challenges and dangers. It clearly delineates the covenant of fate, and it builds the context for the various experiences of destiny met up with.

Yet, Peoplehood as a guiding concept can be problematic in the realm of "destiny" and vision. It can overlook the fact that the existence of the Jews looks beyond ethnicity by building contexts and 'channels' for the variegated *covenants* of destiny in our time. The prophets, we have suggested, understood the peoplehood of Israel as ultimately nourished and even legitimated by the values that make the Jews both a faith community as well as a people. To again cite Buber, the Jews are a nation because a national existence is required to live by the specific religious vision; the Jews are a nation, or, if you will, a people, because the specific religious task of the people of Israel cannot be implemented except by a people. The religious demand is not made to provide the nation with a culture; rather, the nation exists in order to further the vision that the culture makes accessible. Jewish life, annoyingly, thus always has to explain itself. But this is its claim to eternity, and the locale of its vision; the rationale for not simply being like everyone else, for not disappearing.

In this context, Jewish leadership must, in addition to leading the search for Jewish security, serve the Jews in their search for the meaning, the destiny if you will, of Jewish existence. Here there will be no blurring of distinctions but increased efforts of dialogue; pluralism without loss of conviction, learning to see the Jewish sense in the story of a Yehoyachim, restored to a semblance of hope and respect – yet all this without sentimentality or over-spiritualized mystifications.

Finally, an aside, but, I think, very much to the point: I was struck by the decision of *The Jerusalem Report,* surely an instrument addressing itself to the Jewish People and the experiences of Jews, to drop its important feature: "Shabbat Around the World", that provided times for the advent and conclusion of the Sabbath in all major centers of Jewish life. Can there be a more pithy metaphor for Jewish Peoplehood than that feature which, in bare names and numbers, hinted at the drama of the Friday sun, hurtling through space, bringing light to zone after zone, and then, moving away into dusk? This is a sundown greeted by innumerable Sabbath lights, as though to banish the approaching darkness, or if you will, to greet the Sabbath. The Sabbath lights are lit in Jerusalem and Johannesburg, in Tel Aviv and Paris, in New York and Melbourne as the Sabbath, together with the ever setting sun, moves to cover the face of the earth. The associations of 'Shabbat times' touch on Jewish Peoplehood at its core. Is there a better way to point to the drama of Jewish Peoplehood, and the Sabbath entrusted to it "as a perpetual sign", than that late and lamented "Shabbat Around the World" page?

1. This essay is based largely on my "The Problem of Jewish Peoplehood" in Menachem Revivi and Ezra Kopelowitz (eds.) *Jewish Peoplehood: Change and Challenge*, Academic Studies Press, 2008, pp. 12-32. Published here with permission.

2. J.B. Soloveitchik: *"Kol Dodi Dofek* (The Voice of my Beloved Knocks) " in *Ish Ha-emunah (The Man of Faith), Jerusalem:* Mossad Ha-rav Kook, 5731, pp. 86-99

3. Simon Rawidowicz: "Israel: The Ever Dying People", Rawidowicz, *Studies in Jewish Thought*, ed. Nahum Glatzer, Philadelphia: The Jewish Publication Society of America, 1974, pp. 210-224

4. Zeev W. Mankowitz, *Life Between Memory and Hope; The Survivors of the Holocaust in Occupied Germany,* Cambridge UK: Cambridge University Press, 2002, p. 131

5. Mordecai M. Kaplan, *Judaism as a Civilization,* New York: Schocken Books, 1967

6. In conversation with the author.

7. The Mussar movement (the Moralist movement) refers to a Jewish ethical, educational and cultural movement that developed in 19th century Orthodox Eastern Europe, particularly among Lithuanian Jews.

8. R. Moses Sofer, the *Hatam Sofer*

9. Ahad Ha-am, pen name of Asher Zvi Hirsch Ginsberg (1856-1927), was a Hebrew essayist and one of the foremost pre-state Zionist thinkers. He is known as the founder of Cultural Zionism. Yosef Haim Brenner (1881-1921) was a Ukrainian-born renowned iconoclastic author, one of the pioneers of modern Hebrew literature. Abraham Isaac Kook (1865–1935), founder of the Religious Zionist Yeshiva Merkaz HaRav, was a Jewish thinker, Halakhist, Kabbalist and a renowned Torah scholar. Theodor Herzl, (1860-1904) also known as *Hoze Ha'Medinah*, (visionary of the State) was an Austro-Hungarian journalist and the father of

modern political Zionism. Max Simon Nordau (1849-1923), born Simon Maximilian Südfeld, in Hungary, was a Zionist leader, physician, author, and social critic. He was a co-founder of the World Zionist Organization together with Theodor Herzl. For a discussion of these seminal personalities, see Gideon Shimoni, *The Zionist Ideology*, Hanover & London: Brandeis University Press, 1995.

10. Heinrich Graetz, *History of the Jews I*, Philadelphia: The Jewish Publication Society of America, 5717-1956, p. 265

11. Jeremiah 32:15

12. Rev. Dr. I. W. Slotki, Kings, Soncino Press, 1950, p. 324

13. (Vol. 37, No. 4, April 1964); reprinted in Marshall Sklare, "Intermarriage and the Jewish Future", *Observing American Jews*, Hanover, N.H. Brandeis University Press, 1993, pp. 234-247

14. Each kind of *kipah* testifying to a different theology and sociology: the large knitted skullcaps of "Land of Israel" stalwarts, 'peaceniks' with their smaller, usually black knitted *kipot*, haredim with black silky or velvet *kipot*, and more.

15. A quorum of 10 men

16. Eliezer Goldman, "Values and Decisions" *Forum 4 for the Problems of Zionism, Jewry and the State of Israel – Proceedings of the Jerusalem Ideological Conference*, Jerusalem: WZO, 1959, pp. 372-376

17. Ibid.

18. Ibid.

19. Ibid.

20. Note that we have questioned whether what he calls the "irrational element" of that belonging is still as overpowering in the present generation as it was in the past, even in Goldman's generation.

21. Ibid.

22. Ibid., pp. 375-76

23. Martin Buber, "The Jew in the World", Idem, *Israel and the World: Essays in a time of crisis,* New York, Schocken Books, 1963, p. 169

24. Ibid., p. 172

25. "Hebrew Humanism" *Israel and the World,* p. 252

VI

The Jewish Calendar:
Between "Nissan" and "Tishrei"

In this essay, we hope to bring together two value-concepts[1] animating much of Jewish tradition: the *particular* and the *universal*. We shall discuss the connection between the two in the Jewish tradition by way of the festivals of Judaism. Let us note that this essay is specifically designed to address the issue of curriculum with regard to the way the Jewish tradition 'thinks'. For that reason it has a pace and mode of presentation of its own, which reminds us that theology in Judaism deals primarily with concrete questions and instances.

As in any culture, the *unique,* or the particular, refers to those features of culture that place 'our' experiences, problems, hopes and concerns at the center of our visions and consciousness. This consciousness is not necessarily parochial; it may, in fact, lead to deep respect for others who also have their own cultures, memories and aspirations. We may see them as embodying different forms of human experience that we perhaps cannot enter and may never completely understand. We may be fascinated by them, and may even enjoy the variety of human experience to which they bear witness. Yet our 'particular' consciousness and concern bids us to remain loyal to our own ways of doing things. We may even entertain the belief and feeling that 'our' ways are, in some sense, particularly worthy and noble or even commanded, at least for us. This is particularly true in relation to curriculum which deals with our vision of what is truly worthy of being transmitted to our young.

Yet the opposite may also occur. The particularity of 'our' community and culture may at times make us insensitive to what all human beings have in common. We may come to feel that it is only *our* history, *our* community, *our* values that count, that have a monopoly on sense and virtue. When we are blinded to the commonalities we share with others who don't 'belong', who are 'outsiders', we may justifiably be called *radically particularistic*.

As for the *universal*, it refers to the features of a culture or a sensibility that sees human beings, first and foremost, as belonging to the entire human family. The universally-minded person identifies with the human individual, and feels for him or her, wherever and however that individual lives. Universalism demands that we recognize that each culture has vulnerabilities and potentialities that are tied in with those of all other cultures. When we have a universal perspective, we seek to make ourselves communicative to others, to speak fraternally with them, regardless of their community or group identity. However, when we disregard the particular experiences and needs of the community in the name of the universal, so that our – or any – community is arbitrarily excluded from the roster of the historical cultural communities that make up humankind, then our position is *radically universalistic*. Then we disclaim any particular identity and all specific responsibilities that relate to those 'close' to us.

On the one hand, therefore, there are persons who enthusiastically work for the benefit of their group or extended family, who value that collective highly and derive strength and meaning from belonging to it. It is important to them that the group thrives, and they wish to be proud of it. By working hard for the group that is valuable to them, they hope to enhance that value. On the other hand, there are individuals who feel that, in any case of conflict between 'us' and the sum total of humankind, it is always more important to favor the human universe and to be primarily concerned for its welfare. It is assigned the highest value, and no group, certainly not mine, should consider itself as more valuable than 'the family of man' as such.

Holidays as High Drama

How is all this related to festivals? The thesis I am presenting here is that most holidays, across varying cultures, are not only 'days off' but symbolic and even ritualized expressions of values. They have, each in its own way, 'a point to make' about *values* that we are meant to incorporate into our own lives. This is certainly true of holidays that seem most solemn or that are otherwise rich in symbols and in social and public patterns of behaving, and evocative of significant memories. But often it is true even of those that seem quite trivial.

To illustrate, we shall briefly summarize a now classic story by the Canadian humorist, Stephen Leacock, that 'comically' states the case for the connection between values and holidays. The story is entitled "How We Celebrated Mother's Day".[2] It is about a family that decided to make "a real holiday" of Mother's Day by having everyone in the family take off from work and school on that occasion, so as to have a wonderful holiday with Mother, driving through the countryside. It was decided (by Father) that the best way for Mother to enjoy the outing would be to go fishing. He explained that outings were always more fun when they had a destination. Also, Father had just gotten new fishing rods.

At the very last moment before departure, as everybody was getting into the car, it was discovered that there just wasn't enough room for the whole family because the lunch Mother had prepared and the fishing rods took up a great deal of space, and the two girls of the family had brought along their boyfriends. So, after some posturing by some members of the family, including Father, that "they could just as well stay home" or that the idea of their having some fun for a change was "too good to be true," it was finally decided that the best thing for Mother was to stay home, to have a quiet and peaceful day and to prepare dinner for the family in a leisurely fashion. Father even blamed himself for not having realized just how tiring a fishing expedition would have been for Mother. Mother, he proclaimed, simply didn't rest enough.

So Mother stayed home for her delightful rest. And when everyone returned (far later than scheduled so that Mother had to reheat the evening meal a few times) and had a good wash (Mother had laid out towels for everyone) the whole family festively ate the delicious meal she had prepared. (Father fetched the nuts from the side-board at dessert time to express his determination that Mother not work too hard on 'her day'.) And after Mother had finished washing up, she was heard to admit that it had been the most wonderful day of her life. "And I think," notes the narrator, one of Mother's children, "there were tears in her eyes."

Leacock is reminding us that even Mother's Day is meant to celebrate some value that we are to live by throughout the year. If we cherish Mother for "all that she has done for us" day in and day out, it is appropriate that one day of the year will mark our appreciation and celebrate our value of expressing love and gratitude. But in the family Leacock is describing, Mother is obviously not appreciated or taken seriously on any day of the year. She is a caretaker, verbally and ostentatiously placed on a pedestal on 'her' day. She is not intrinsically valued in her family; she is not really important as a person. No one in the family feels morally or otherwise obligated to her. When the day that celebrates (the value of) 'love for Mother' comes around, it merely reflects the sad state of the family, the absence of the value that the family is supposedly celebrating.

Leacock is saying that there is no point in celebrating a value that is not actively present throughout the year; that there is no chance that the value will 'come alive' by being formally, superficially and sentimentally given lip service for a day. After all, the idea is not to be 'nice' to Mother on one particular day. Rather, it is to set aside a special occasion for a celebration of some value that makes demands on us throughout the year. That special occasion,

225

through its symbols and rituals, educates us to re-examine our loyalty to a specific value and to persevere in it. But what isn't done all year won't miraculously 'happen' on Mother's Day either. In fact, on that special day, the value will be laughably (hence sadly) conspicuous by its absence. No wonder that were tears in Mother's eyes.

Festivals as Channels for Curriculum

Of course, holidays are not *only* valuative pointers. They are much more. They help us to make order of the weeks, months and years of our lives. They place us within nature, helping us into and out of its seasonal changes. They position us within history, and help us participate in its great moments. They are high drama, offering us modes of rejoicing, of anticipation, of mourning – and connecting all these to events that we may re-enact. We see ourselves as having left Egypt on Passover; standing at Mount Sinai on Shavuot; trying to gain a fresh perspective on ourselves on Rosh Hashanah, the New Year; reliving the pageantry at the High Priest's celebration of atonement on Yom Kippur; and re-imagining a desert-wandering in tabernacles on Succot. The calendar, every calendar, is a thorough mix of memories, anxieties, intimations of salvation, getting away from the everyday. But in the Jewish tradition most pointedly, the value being celebrated, or profaned by neglect, is always a central feature of what is going on.

Sages and prophets who taught Judaism as a religious and moral doctrine and path, never tired of making that point. The Shabbat, says Isaiah, is a day of "delight" when

226

it is made "holy to the Lord". Shabbat celebrates the key value of *kedushah* (sanctity). Hence it is celebrated by a "separation" from the mundane and its routines of achievement: of work, competition, 'making it'. But if there is no holiness in daily life, expressed in the innumerable decisions we are always making about what is truly important to us and what is trivial, and in the mix of spontaneity and self-control in our lives, the Sabbath becomes meaningless and tedious. If we do not speak the language of its values, we cannot hear what it is saying and we resent the static it creates by its 'oppressive' rules.

Isaiah, in the prophetic reading the rabbis assigned for the morning of Yom Kippur (57:14 - 58:14), denounces value-less celebration, no matter how seemingly respectable. In this *Haftarah* the prophet expresses biting contempt for the hypocritical and empty observance of the holiest day of the Jewish year. As he describes it, the people are "dutifully" fasting and even mechanically beating their breasts in seeming contrition. And so they feel justified in complaining: "why has God not taken note of our breast-beating, of our fasting and praying?"

The prophet responds in what is surely the classic 'Yom Kippur sermon'. God, he declares, takes no interest in their festival of empty penitential performance. He knows that they "smite their breasts with the fist of wickedness". The divine sarcasm in Isaiah's rebuke is bitter and pained:

> Is such the fast that I have chosen? For a man to afflict his soul? Is it to bow down his head as a bulrush and to spread sackcloth and ashes under him? Will you call this a fast and an acceptable day to the Lord?

> [Rather] Is not this the fast that I have chosen? To
> loose the fetters of wickedness, to undo the bands of
> the yoke, and to let the oppressed go free and that
> you break every yoke? Is it not to deal your bread
> to the hungry? And that you bring the poor who are
> cast out to your house? When you see the naked, that
> you clothe him, and not hide yourself from your own
> flesh? (*Isaiah 58:3-7*)

This passage seems radically universalistic. Forget, the
prophet seems to be saying, the 'rituals' of your own
community. They cannot help you to get the ear of the
universal God. Rather, do what every human being is
obligated to do and what every human being needs: to
give – and receive – freedom; to feed and to be fed; to
give shelter to the homeless and to be brought out of the
street; to clothe and to be clothed. That is the value of Yom
Kippur, what it really means and demands.

But actually, it isn't that clear. Was the prophet against
Jewish 'ritual' or against its hypocritical use? Is he saying
that all must be succored or, at least first of all, "your own
flesh"? We shall return to these issues in due course as we
investigate the universal and particular values of the Jewish
calendar. For this investigation we shall require a key, a
conceptual tool that helps us to decode these universal and
particular values. Yet, before looking for a key to the values
of the Jewish calendar as particular and universal, we might
briefly re-visit that calendar.

A Walk Through the Luach

Judaism's *luach* (calendar) is one of weeks, by virtue of the weekly Sabbath, and of months, because of the festive and other special days that punctuate them. It is a lunar calendar of twelve months, and of thirteen in leap years; the leap years are meant to keep it in line with the solar year. A prominent reason for that is that the three pilgrim festivals, of Pesach, Shavuot and Succot, are, among other things, festivals of harvest: of grain, of first fruits and of the "final ingathering". They have to make their appearances at the appropriate seasons.

The key months of the Jewish calendar are Nissan, the month of spring, and Tishrei, at the approach of autumn. The spring month of Nissan is the first month of the year, but strangely, Tishrei, the seventh, begins with Rosh Hashanah, the New Year. The apparent reason is that cosmic beginnings are seen by the Talmudic sages as connected to moral and religious beginnings and renewals. Repentance is viewed as a kind of self-making, an ascent to greater human holiness. And the seventh month, Tishrei, is the holiest of months, just as the seventh day is the holiest day of the week.

The holiest days of the holy seventh month are Rosh Hashanah, the New Year, and Yom Kippur, the festival of Atonement on the tenth of that month. Then, on the fifteenth of Tishrei begins the seven-day long festival of Succot which is immediately followed by Shemini Atzeret and Simchat Torah, the Eighth Day Concluding Festival.[3]

Despite the special 'awe' associated with Rosh Hashanah and Yom Kippur, the calendar appears to find its organizing principle in the three pilgrim festivals (actually four, with Shemini Atzeret) of "ascent" to the Temple in Jerusalem. And here, Nissan and Tishrei are focal. At full moon in Nissan begins the seven-day long[4] Pesach festival; at full moon in Tishrei, there is the seven day long Succot festival. Seven weeks after Pesach, following "the counting of the Omer" from the second evening of Passover when the first offering of new grain – the Omer – was brought to the Temple, comes the festival of Shavuot. This one day holiday[5] celebrates, at least in its Talmudic interpretation, the Revelation at Mount Sinai. Yet the Talmud calls this festival Atzeret, the "conclusion" of Pesach. And, as mentioned, one day after Succot, (still in Tishrei) comes the pilgrim festival of Shemini Atzeret. Perhaps, one midrash suggests, this festival of Atzeret (conclusion) should, like Shavuot which comes seven weeks after the major Nissan festival, have been celebrated seven weeks after the major Tishrei festival (Succot). But that, in Eretz Yisrael, would have brought Shemini Atzeret into the season when the farmer is praying for plentiful rain and when "the roads are troublesome" (*Yalkut Shimoni, Pinchas* 782). Would a pilgrim festival, at the end of Heshvan (November) not have dampened the farmer's desire for rain, so that he could make it to Jerusalem without getting soaked? Clearly, a conflict of interests!

A Controversy about the Month of Redemption

The Talmud, perhaps even more than the Bible, determines how Jews have perceived their faith and culture. And the *luach,* the calendar, is part and parcel of that. If the Bible mentions Shavuot only in connection with the counting of [the] Omer, and the presentation of loaves in the Temple, the Talmudic sages insist that it is actually *zman matan Toratainu,* "the time of the giving of our Torah", and that *that* is what Jews traditionally celebrate. If the Talmud tells us not to sound the Shofar on Rosh Hashanah when it falls on a Sabbath or not to wave the lulav and the rest of the "four species" on the first day of Succot when it is a Sabbath, that is what we do (or refrain from doing), even though the Torah calls Rosh Hashanah the day of shofar sounding *(yom teru'a)* and obligates "taking the [four species] in hand" on the first day of the festival.

So it is to the Talmudic rabbis we turn to decode our subject and our question: What are values associated with the festivals of Judaism? Are they particular or universal? Do they ignore the universal, the human as such, or do they transcend concern with the particular identity and the particular community of Judaism?

A key to our problem seems to lie hidden within a controversy, recorded in the Talmudic tractate, *Rosh Hashanah,* between two second century sages, Rabbi Eliezer and Rabbi Yehoshua. Listening in on them, we hear a seemingly strange and esoteric discussion as to whether the world was created in Nissan or Tishrei; whether the forefathers were born in the former or the latter month; in which month Joseph was released from prison, and when the oppression in Egypt ceased and messianic redemption will commence. Here is the heart of their discussion:

Rabbi Eliezer says: In [the month of] Tishrei the world was created, in Tishrei the patriarchs [Abraham and Jacob] were born and in Tishrei they died, [though] Isaac was born on Pesach. On Rosh Hashanah, Sarah, Rachel and Hannah were remembered [by God, who promised them children]; on Rosh Hashanah Joseph left prison; on Rosh Hashanah the slave labor of our forefathers in Egypt ceased; *in Nissan [Israel] was redeemed [but] they will in the future be redeemed in Tishrei.*

Rabbi Yehoshua says: The world was created in [the month of] Nissan, the patriarchs were born in Nissan and in Nissan they died and on Pesach Isaac was born. On Rosh Hashanah Sarah, Rachel and Hannah were remembered; on Rosh Hashanah, Joseph left prison; on Rosh Hashanah the slave labor of our ancestors ceased. *In Nissan they [Israel] were redeemed and their future redemption will [likewise] be in Nissan.*

(Rosh Hashanah 10b-11a)

This conversation, which continues with various proof texts cited by Rabbi Eliezer and Rabbi Yehoshua to buttress their positions, is surely not simply an attempt to 'get at the facts'. Nor is this a case of simple conjecture or prediction. They are trying to tell us something about the Jewish view of the nature of things and about the world of value.

We have to keep in mind that the Talmudic teachers did not follow the Greek model of discourse wherein concepts were expressed by way of abstract terms, such as Justice,

Beauty, and Reason. Rather, they preferred terms taken from the world of concrete experience. When speaking of damages, they refer us to goring oxen and unguarded pits; when discussing the reasons for the destruction of the Temple, they link the catastrophe to a dinner party in which the host insulted his guest, because "the Temple was destroyed as a result of baseless hatred".[6] So too: Nissan and Tishrei in our controversy certainly represent more than months of the year, though they are that as well. They are pointers to aspects of spiritual reality. Thus, we must try to decipher why even Rabbi Yehoshua, with his 'Nissan particularistic orientation', agrees that the sufferings of our physically oppressed ancestors ceased on Rosh Hashanah (in Tishrei) as did the mental affliction of three childless women, and also, the confinement of Joseph. What can we learn from the fact that all these persons suffered indignities that bring into view human vulnerabilities, species of sufferings that in principle are no different for Gentiles than for Jews?

Our two Sages cannot agree when the world was created or when the patriarchs were born or died, though both agree that Isaac was born on Pesach (Nissan).[7] Does this assignation of the patriarch Isaac's birthday indicate that there are different characteristics and orientations to be attached to Abraham and Jacob than to Isaac? And what difference does it make whether the final redemption will be in Nissan or in Tishrei? Having waited so long, why should six months matter to us?

Nissan and Tishrei

What do Nissan and Tishrei represent? What they have in common is that they are both festive seasons. But how do they differ?

Nissan, of course, is the month of the Exodus, when we sit down at the Seder table to recount and recall the dramatic epic of Israel's redemption. God sent Moses to "take us out" but Pharaoh was "stiff-necked" and so ten plagues were brought upon Egypt. The Israelites had to place blood on their doorposts so that the destroying angel would *pass over* their houses when he smote the first-born of Egypt. And then there is the splitting of the Red Sea. Israel passes through the Sea in dry safety while the pursuing Egyptian hosts are drowned in the resurgent waters. Whereupon the Israelites sing a Song of Praise and Deliverance. The Talmudic teachers state that the angels too began to sing a song of praise, whereupon God sternly rebuked them: "[As] the works of My hands are drowning in the sea, you sing songs of praise?" (*Sanhedrin* 39b) (The Israelites are rightfully grateful for their salvation; they have earned the right to sing. But you were not thus threatened.) Nissan, we see, is blatantly the month of particularism.

Compare that redemption with the festive month of Tishrei, beginning with Rosh Hashana, the New Year, that the Talmud calls the "Day of Remembrance", and the day of creation (according to Rabbi Eliezer). On that day, the Jewish tradition pictures God to be judging the world, calling on all humankind to acknowledge His sovereignty, to turn and return to Him in truth and justice. As "the first day of Creation", it invites to new beginnings, to repentance and soul-searching.

There follows Yom Kippur, the solemn day of divine forgiveness. A paradigm story for what Yom Kippur represents is the short Book of Jonah, read during the afternoon service (minchah) of that day. Jonah is sent by God to the Gentile city of Ninveh, to tell the people there of their impending destruction. Yet when the people of Ninveh repent of their transgressions, God repeals His decree. Unlike what happened to the Egyptians (and their horses) in Nissan, the Ninve'ites of Tishrei, their six score thousand persons that "cannot discern between their right hand and their left hand" (i.e., children) and even their cattle win God's compassion.

And then, the festival of Succot. Biblically, Succot commemorates God's Providence over Israel during its wandering in the desert. Yet the tendency of the tradition, drawing on biblical themes, is to interpret it as symbolizing aspects of the human condition and the aspiration for universal redemption. The reading of the somber Book of Ecclesiastes on Succot, which speaks of the "vanity" of everything but for the performance of God's commandments, suggests a comprehensive view of the sorry human situation and the redemptive quality of the spiritual and responsible life, not only for Israel, but for humankind as a whole. In this scheme of things, the sukkah, as a providential shelter, is also a symbol of the precariousness of human life, a "wandering" throughout life and history. In line with the element of salvation that Succot represents, it makes sense that the final apocalyptic war of history, of Gog and Magog, is associated with Succot,[8] and that the processions in the ancient Temple and even in contemporary synagogues with the "four species" are accompanied with prayers and psalms for and of salvation: *Ana HaShem Hoshia Na* (Please, O Lord, Save), *Hosha Na, l'ma'ancha E-lohainu, Hosha Na* (Please Save, for Your sake, our God, save!). Surely, a ceremony and declaration of clear Messianic overtones. The Talmudic sages understand the seventy offerings presented on the altar during Succot to represent the "seventy nations of the world", who do not themselves "ascend" to Jerusalem before Messianic times, so that Israel has to pray for atonement on their behalf, and pray for their peace.[9] Nor does it seem accidental that King Solomon chose to dedicate the Temple on Succot. And note that Solomon, after declaring how Israel will call upon God's name and praying that God will answer their prayers, adds:

> Also, concerning the stranger who is not of Your people when he shall come from a distant land for Your name's sake – for they [in those lands] will hear of Your great name and of Your mighty hand and of Your outstretched arm – when [this stranger] will come and pray towards this house [the Temple], hear You in heaven, Your dwelling place, and do all that the stranger asks of You so that all the peoples of the earth may know Your name, to stand in awe of You, as does Your people Israel and that they may know that Your name is called upon this house that I have built. (*I Kings* 8:41-43)

We see, then, that the controversy between Rabbi Eliezer and Rabbi Yehoshua is not simply about ascertaining dates or "locating" the redemption within the calendar. Nissan seems to represent a kind of festival, hence also, a certain view of the world. "Nissan" confronts us with certain ideas of what is important, and the values by which we should live our lives. The Nissan particularistic orientation is born out of the need of our people to be itself, to define itself, to find its own freedom. If, as Rabbi Yehoshua believed, the world was created in Nissan, then this particularity of each group is "natural"; it is in tune with what God created the world to be. In this approach, the fact that the patriarchs were born and died "in Nissan", means that throughout their lives they were, first and foremost, architects of their people, nation-builders. When that vocation required confrontation with others, even warfare, or lack of contact with others, even seclusion from them, these men of Nissan were up to the challenge and not torn by it. In the case of Isaac, who according to both opinions was born in Nissan, the withdrawal from the wider world was self-understood. Isaac, we recall, never left the Land of Israel and when he wished to escape famine by going to Egypt as his father Abraham had done, God succinctly tells him: "[You shall] reside in this land" (Genesis 26:3). Isaac was a bridge between Abraham and Jacob: he "kept the birth of the nation of Israel going" and without the fanfare or drama of his father's or his son's lives, laid the foundations for Jewish roots and rootedness.

Both of our Sages agree that the initial redemption of Israel took place in Nissan. The salvation of Israel in Egypt

Michael Rosenak

was at the expense of the Egyptians. There was oppression and then plagues, finally, pursuit, violent confrontation, a war situation. In wartime, there is little opportunity to think of the enemy as a human being, much like yourself, who needs and deserves the same consideration and compassion as you do.

As we have seen, our rabbis also disagree about the Messianic redemption of the future. Rabbi Yehoshua seems to be afraid that a future redemption of Tishrei may be too universal for comfort. If redemption is a universalistic conception, may it not involve the disappearance of Israel? Will not many, perhaps like some early Christians he may have known, proclaim the Messianic time as not requiring the survival of Israel? Perhaps it is because of such fears that he insists that the redemption must be, first and foremost, a particular change of fortune for Israel.

Rabbi Eliezer disagrees. The ultimate redemption must be universal. Can Israel consider itself really redeemed when the rest of the world is not? Should the physically enslaved of the world not hear the voice of Rosh Hashanah that proclaims the end of their suffering? Yet despite all this, why would Rabbi Eliezer not fear the philosophical universalists that flourished even in his own time, who foretold that the redemption will and must bring about the demise of Israel?

A further look at the calendar may give us an inkling of why Rabbi Eliezer was not worried. For, in fact, in the Jewish tradition that such teachers as Rabbi Eliezer and Rabbi Yehoshua have shaped for us, Nissan and Tishrei are never to be found in isolation. Even for Rabbi Yehoshua, the salvation of human beings as such is grounded in the universal experience that Tishrei represents: fulfillment as mothers, liberation from confinement, deliverance from slavery. And even for Rabbi Eliezer, Nissan remains present, both in the Exodus from Egypt, (the paradigmatic national liberation), and in the character and teaching of the patriarch Isaac, the one who cultivates the inwardness, the separate identity, of Israel.

Where Nissan and Tishrei Meet

In fact, our calendar features a constant interplay of Nissan and Tishrei, the 'particular' and the 'universal', on two levels. There is, first of all, the restraint on a radical Nissan or Tishrei approach imposed on the Nissan and Tishrei pilgrim festivals (Pesach and Shavuot) by their respective *Atzeret* (concluding) holidays (Shavuot and Shemini Atzeret). Also, there is an interplay between "Nissan" and "Tishrei" in the Pesach and Succot paradigms themselves. Let us look at each category in turn:

Two Satellite Festivals:

1 – Shavuot and Shemini Atzeret

In the Talmudic tradition, Shavuot is mainly about the revelation of the Torah, tied to Pesach by "the counting of the Omer" which symbolizes the impatience of the liberated Israelites to receive the Torah, the goal of their freedom. Yet, unlike their liberation, their receiving of the Torah is largely, perhaps mainly, a Tishrei event. The Torah is about obedience and constraint; it redefines identity as requiring holiness; it redefines freedom as the service of God. It is thus a paradigm of the ideal of all humankind as God intended in His creation of it. After all, it was what he intended for Adam and Eve! No wonder that a famous midrash describes Him going from nation to nation, asking them whether they would accept the Torah.[10] Perhaps this 'peddling' of the Torah was tongue-in-cheek (for when each asked what the Torah commands, God, in each case, told them what they least wished to hear). Yet, the Torah tells us that the covenant of commandment was given to all humans long before Sinai in what are called the seven Noahide commandments. Indeed, the ancient Book of Jubilees, perhaps the first to refer specifically to Shavuot as the time of revelation, states:

> And it was written in the Heavenly Tablets that the Feast of Shavuot be celebrated in this month, once a year to renew the covenant (between Noah and God, that there will be no more flood). (*Jubilees* 6:15-22)

Furthermore, the Torah, say the rabbis, was given in the desert that belongs to no nation so that none, not even Israel, could claim exclusive possession of it. And the Torah, teaches a midrash, was spoken on Mount Sinai in seventy languages, corresponding to the "seventy nations" that constitute humanity. (Recall the seventy offerings of Succot.)

Yet the centerpiece of the 'Tishrei character' of Nissan's concluding festival is surely the Book of Ruth, the story of a Moabite woman who turned to the God of Israel, whose individual character and heroism 'undid' the biblical 'Nissan-type' prohibition on Moabites and Amorites entering the community of Israel. The writer of Ruth tell us that she was the great-grandmother of the Messiah but the Midrash gives her, if possible, even greater cosmic significance: The day that this granddaughter of Balak, the king of Moab who wished only to curse Israel, accepted the Torah, says the midrash,[11] is comparable with the day that Israel stood at Mount Sinai.

Shemini Atzeret, the concluding festival of Tishrei's Succot, takes on a decidedly 'Nissan-like' character in our tradition. The midrashic sages who point out that seventy sacrifices were offered on Succot on behalf of the nations of the world, note that on Shemini Atzeret, only one bullock was offered for Israel itself. The Talmud portrays Shemini Atzeret, which has no 'reason' given in the Torah for its observance at all, as an intimate get-together between God and Israel (*Sukkah* 55b). Shemini Atzeret is also the day of *tefillat geshem*, the prayer for rain, as the rainy season approaches in Eretz Yisrael. [As an aside: The 'particularity' of that prayer, its Nissan-like character, was well expressed by the late Leon (Aryeh) Dulchin, one-time head of the Jewish Agency for Israel. Dulchin once related that he became a Zionist as a child in Mexico City, on Shemini Atzeret. The people of Mexico City are fond of saying that their city has four seasons each day, one of which is invariably rainy. On that particular Shemini Atzeret day, Aryeh and his father were coming out of the synagogue, after having recited the prayer for rain, into a veritable downpour. Whereupon Dulchin asked his father: "Why do we pray for rain? It rains all the time!" To which his father responded, in Yiddish: "Laibele, *dos ist nisht unser regen* (Leon, this isn't our rain)!"]

But the main claim of Shemini Atzeret to honorary Nissan-status is surely based on what happened to its second (Diaspora) day in the early Middle Ages in Babylonia, namely that it was re-invented as Simchat Torah. There, it became customary to conclude the yearly cycle of Torah reading on that day and to immediately return to the beginning, all this in the intimate association with God that the midrash ascribed to the mood of Shemini Atzeret. There was dancing, processions (*hakafot*), revelry, outpourings of love and enthusiasm for the Torah. It was as if to say: for us, the year begun on Rosh Hashanah as a cosmic universal event does not really begin until we have begun reading our Torah anew.

This was a different type of Torah celebration than Shavuot, which was all about revelation, about seeking enlightenment from texts in all-night vigils of study, about being changed by Torah. Simchat Torah has been about being Jewish, just being able to hold the Torah and participate in the drama of ending and beginning it, enjoying every minute and being who you are! And it still is that way, even in Israel, where Simchat Torah seems at times to crowd out the more solemn festival of Shmini Atzeret with its *tefillat geshem* and the recitation of *yiskor* in memory of the deceased, by 'falling' vibrantly, even boisterously, on the very same day.

2 – *Particularism and Universalism once again*

Just as the concluding festivals of Pesach and Succot balance the orientations of Nissan and Tishrei, so do these holidays themselves exist in constant tension between the particularism that is Nissan and the universalism that is Tishrei. On Pesach, the entire *Hallel* (psalms of praise) are recited only on the first day[12]; thereafter, we remove two psalms and recite what is called 'half-*Hallel*', traditionally seen as marking a measure of distress at the destruction of the Egyptians. For the same reason, we remove a drop of wine from the Seder cup upon reciting the plagues on the Seder evening. How can we say that "our cup runneth over" while human beings are suffering? Most importantly, no leaven may be eaten on Pesach, the festival of freedom. Leavened bread, Hasidic masters point out, puffs itself up. National liberation, 'making it', triumph, are heady affairs. All too often they inflate collective egos, what the perpetrators of such puffing up like to call 'justifiable pride' often achieved at the expense of seeing the reality and the suffering of the other. Pesach, literally achieved through blood and thunder, educates us through its ritual to incorporate a Tishrei element even into the festive pride of Nissan. Matzah is always lowly, more suitable for slaves than for lords. It is the "bread of affliction" that our enslaved ancestors ate in Egypt.

The historical satellites of Nissan and Pesach, are Hanukkah and Purim and, in our days, Yom Atzma'ut (Israel Independence Day) and Yom Yerushalayim (Jerusalem Day).[13] They are festive occasions of national salvation, associated with war – and victory. Yet they too confront the problematic presence of Tishrei as a moral and religious dimension of Judaism. On Hanukkah, the victory over "the Greeks" is celebrated with oil lamps; on Purim, the foiling of Haman who wished to kill all the Jews, with sending "portions" of cake and wine to friends and gifts to the poor, and sometimes, by getting drunk at the happiness of deliverance and at the sad recognition that this is not a world one can always bear to look at while sober. Yom Atzma'ut, the dominant Nissan-event-celebration of our days is marked by picnics, a Bible quiz, and other cultural events. So far, one may see little of Tishrei on Jerusalem Day. Therefore, we do not know as yet how it will fare. Will it be a kind of latter day Hanukkah, or a modern Yom Nikkanor, a celebration of Maccabean victory that the Talmudic sages gently discarded?

On the Sabbath of Hannukah, when we celebrate the might of the Maccabees, we read the prophecy of Zechariah[14] who declares: "Not by force and not by might, says the Lord of Hosts but by My spirit." On Yom Ha'atzmaut it is customary to read a prophetic passage, a Haftarah, as well. It is from Isaiah 10-11, and describes Messianic times. Its perhaps most famous passage is pure "Tishrei":

> They shall not hurt nor destroy
> On all My holy mountain;
> For the earth shall be full of the knowledge of the Lord;
> As the waters cover the sea. (*Isaiah* 11:9)

If Nissan does not lack characteristics of Tishrei, neither does Tishrei lack Nissan traits. Succot is 'odd' to non-Jews; the exit from comfortable modern homes to a 'hut' for seven days in particular strikes many non-Jews as eccentric.[15]

Succot, as anyone reading the Haftarah of "the war of Gog and Magog" will see, is not devoid of what we may call the dark side of redemption: namely, the destruction or humiliation of the wicked, associated in most cases with 'the other', who epitomizes what is wrong with the (unredeemed) world.

Succot incorporates Nissan in another way as well: Michael Strassfield, after dwelling on the universal aspect of Succot, touches on a bit of Nissan consciousness, the gloomy side of it:

> ...the sukkah, while evoking the image of God sheltering us in the future, raises another, opposing image: The sukkah as a temporary structure open to the winds of autumn cannot help but remind us of the Jewish people's experience of the last 2000 years of exile and wandering. Are we not the prototypical alien – the wandering Jew? Are not the forty years in the desert – the period Sukkot commemorates – the archetype of our 2000 years of wandering?
>
> The sukkah, then, evokes opposing sets of images: rootlessness and home, wandering and return, exposure and shelter. Just as matzah is both slave bread and free bread, the sukkah stands for the contrary realities of our lives.[16]

Michael Rosenak

The Architecture of Jewish Life: Festivals and Values

Nissan and Tishrei suggest not only views of the world that interact, but values for Jewish life that are to be 'celebrated' throughout the year, on Sabbaths and festivals. Nissan is not only a statement about the particularity of many aspects of our complex reality, but an invitation to see the concrete existence of the Jewish people as important, as *value*-able, as requiring participation through remembering, experiencing and striving. This particularity is not to be confused with arrogance or indifference to others: at the height of our celebration of *our* freedom we recall God's rebuke to the singing angels who may be expected to be universal in their sympathies.

We are brought back to thinking about our freedom when commanded not to oppress the stranger, "for you know the heart of the stranger, having been slaves in Egypt" (Exodus 23:9). To be particular in our celebration of Pesach is to express our uniqueness, by binding ourselves to God, who freed us, in the words of the Pesach Haggadah, to "draw us to His service". We indeed may believe that the way we celebrate our freedom, through the strict ritual regimen of Pesach, is a particularly worthy and educative way, but this does not require us to denigrate others or to deny our own ignoble past – as slaves.

We are called upon to 'do' Nissan every day: in defense of our heritage, perhaps as soldiers of the Israel Defense Forces, when searching for ourselves in the process of learning our texts, and when literally or figuratively dancing with our Torah. We are asked to be loyal yet critical; for without critique our culture and our institutions will lose their vitality and become less compelling. Whether on festivals or weekdays, we are bidden to rejoice when Jews rejoice, and to mourn together. Nissan asks us to speak our own language, and not to be put off by what others consider 'peculiar' about us – even when, in the tussle between Nissan and Tishrei, our syntax seems immediately problematic and thus challenging. We are not to be alienated. And, as Rabbi Yehoshua would insist, we are not to disparage redemptive events and developments, particularly the existence of the State of Israel, just because they have not yet redeemed the world. After the Holocaust, even the 'mere' redemption of Nissan looks good and tastes sweet.

Nissan suggests that while we should feel for all humankind and extend help whenever and wherever possible – for all suffering is ultimately an individual, a Tishrei, phenomenon – yet those close to us, "the poor of our own city" take precedence. One who is committed to 'everyone' generally forgets that his or her children are first in line when it comes to schooling, listening – and replacing worn-out shoes. Nissan is suspicious of people it perceives as loving 'the family of man' more than their own families. Nissan does not see Isaiah decrying fasting and praying, but only as mocking the false and hypocritical ways these actions are sometimes carried out. And Nissan understands why the prophet urged his listeners not to hide from the needs of "your own flesh". Our own 'flesh', our own community, are our immediate responsibility.

Rabbi Eliezer does not deny the claims of Nissan but insists on a Tishrei perspective. (Would Abraham and

Jacob have been able to persist as Tishrei people without the solid stay-at-home figure of Isaac? Would Israel still be around to envision Tishrei without the Nissan redemption from Egypt?) Ultimately, he says, the very Nissan character of the Jewish, indeed, of any, tradition, is that it is to find itself within a world created in Tishrei. For Judaism, this means that its Nissan characteristics, i.e., being a distinct and unique people, must in the final analysis be seen in the perspective of its universal monotheistic faith. True, redemptions of Nissan are worthy, but one must be wary about how one celebrates them: one may not smugly have one's 'cup running over' when others are suffering. A Simchat Torah (Nissan) that does not hear the Shavuot (Tishrei) decision of that stranger, Ruth, is too boisterous. A celebration of the State of Israel on Yom Atzma'ut that imposes a curfew on Palestinian Arabs for thirty six hours has to be based on security considerations alone; otherwise, Tishrei insists, Yom Atzma'ut simply exposes Nissan's dangerous potential for emptiness and false sentimentality. Then Nissan stands to lose its redemptive character.

Tishrei wishes the symbols and practices of Judaism to be seen, also, as symbolic and social anticipations of the Messianic world that is the goal of Jewish history. Rabbi Eliezer seems unconcerned that Tishrei will melt us away in the unity of humankind. He is aware of the interplay of Nissan and Tishrei. So, he would not have us simply reflect on the tension between Providence and homelessness, between the courage to go on and the certainty of God's salvation. Rather, he would insist that we do our primary reflection while sitting in the sukkah and shaking a lulav.

Unlike Rabbi Yehoshua he thinks there is an inherent aspect of reality that makes this possible and natural, for "the world was created in Tishrei". Certainly he would insist that, despite the importance of the redemption of Nissan, it is all leading to a redemption of Tishrei, still to come.

It seem plausible that Rabbi Yehoshua would agree, while insisting that even in the future redemption, Israel's hold on reality be assured by its *own* redemption, say, its return to its land. For doesn't he himself say that the end of tribulations, the coming out from situations of affliction and moving towards freedom and fulfillment, unfettered, first took place on Rosh Hashanah? To a large degree, the Jewish curriculum makes it possible for Jewish learners to understand, literally, this insight – and that this all has to do with universalism and particularism (among other things), through the prism of Jewish teaching.

---

1. Value-concept is a term suggested by Max Kadushin in his pioneering work on Talmudic thinking, *The Rabbinic Mind*, New York: JTSA, 1952.

2. Stephen Leacock, *Laugh with Leacock: An Anthology of the Best Work of Stephen Leacock*, Dodd, Mead, 1981. A slightly different version of the story is available at http://www.lovetolearn.net/mothersdaystory/

3. Two days in the Diaspora. It would be interesting to study how many Jews have moved to Israel in the last fifty years and more to save themselves and their children the 'problem' of Tishrei, of going or not going to school, and of working or not working on the seven days of festival (in the Diaspora) in that special month.

Also, for how many young people has the problem has been
solved by study at Jewish Day Schools?

4. Eight in the Diaspora

5. Two days in the Diaspora

6. B.T. Gittin, 55B-56A

7. This is strange: common sense would have suggested that he be
born in Tishrei, one year after the angels promised Sarah a child,
and not a mere six months after! After all, they place this divine
promise to Sarah on Rosh Hashanah!

8. See the Haftarot of the first day and of the Shabbat of the
Intermediate days – *Shabbat Chol Hamoed*

9. See Rashi, *Bamidbar 29:38*

10. Midrash Sifre on Deut. 33:2

11. *Nazir* 23b

12. Or first two, in the Diaspora

13. The major fast day of the calendar, Tisha b'Av, the day of the
destruction of the Temple, is obviously anchored in Nissan as
well, but anticipates the coming of the Messiah. Rabbi Eliezer
might say, then, that even Tisha B'Av looks towards 'Tishrei'.
(This does not include Yom Kippur which enjoys the status of
"High Holiday" in the Jewish tradition, despite being a day of
abstinence from food

14. Zechariah 3:6

15. The Talmud, [*Avodah Zarah 3a-b*] wishing to spoof the Gentiles
who desire Israel's status as a divinely elected people, are
told that this status derives entirely from the observance of
God's commandments. God thereupon gives them a "simple"
commandment to fulfill, the sukkah. But when God raises the heat
to summer heights, they give up on the sukkah in disgust.

16. Michael Strassfeld, *The Jewish Holidays: A Guide and Commentary*,
New York: Harper and Row, 1985, p. 147

In Lieu of an Epilogue

From the Minsker and Pinsker to our two Talmudic
teachers with whom we have just studied, we have traveled
a considerable, albeit abbreviated, journey, and listened in
on a number of conversations. Now the question may be
asked whether, in modern Jewish consciousness, there is
still room for these types of conversations about God and
the presence of God. Can people of our time still conduct
such conversations or only, at best, listen in on them?
Where could Jews today stand on the subjects we have
raised here?

This book has touched on a range of questions
concerning Jewish life and learning in today's world, and
ponders the issue of whether traditional historical answers
can stand up to new challenges and novel questions. What
are Jewish sensibilities in the modern world, and what are
the forms in which they are expressed? Do learning and
religious observance still enjoy the same priority they once
had? And what in fact do we mean by 'learning' and what
do we mean by piety and devotion?

Ludwig Lewisohn – the American Jewish writer – once
told a tale of a band of post-World War II Jewish refugees
who, while fleeing from the Soviet army, came to the
deserted and bombed-out house which had been the home
of one of them before the great destruction. Searching
amongst the rubble, this man found a stray page of Talmud,

wet and soiled. To the amazement of his fellow survivors, he sat down "to study". Aghast, they shouted that time was short; the Soviets were at their heels. "Sha," he said, "m'darf lernen!" [Quiet! One must learn!]

In today's cultural context, is this a story that arouses discernment and understanding about Jewish life and perhaps even about one's Jewish self, or are we too far removed from all that? Questions such as these have preoccupied us here.

* * *

In closing the deliberations raised in these essays, I recall an incident that occurred a few years ago that seems to speak to the concern illustrated by the episode I related about my father at the beginning of our journey – that of continuing Jewish fellowship, integrity and trust.

Several years ago, my family celebrated the bar mitzvah of one of my grandchildren. This was not an ordinary bar mitzvah because the beloved mother of the chief celebrant was terminally ill. As might be expected, we were all in a state of deep emotional turmoil as we were both celebrating and taking leave. On the afternoon preceding the bar mitzvah, I tried to gather my thoughts to compose "a word of Torah" that would be relevant and worth saying – and trustworthy.

In a gesture of reverence – and habit – I opened a volume of Midrash Rabbah, a rabbinic commentary on the Torah, to seek some enlightenment. To my astonishment, from the volume a little piece of paper fluttered to the ground, and when I picked it up, I saw that it was a commentary that my grandfather had prepared in honor of the bar mitzvah of *his* son (my father)! Even more astounding, it spoke most poignantly to me in this hour of celebration-and-distress – of tradition and transmission, of trust through turbulence, and of "going on" in the midst of chaos and seeming meaninglessness.

On the personal level, this story, like my story of my handkerchief, has invited me to theological reflection. But not all theological reflections are personal and some take place on a collective level as well. This may indeed be perceived by many as the primary level. In either case, the stories suggest significance, but do not generally dictate it.

I suggest that in this secular era too, perhaps surprisingly, there is still testimony and there is truth, and we are invited to find truth in the testimony that presents itself to us and that is continually unfolding before our eyes. This testimony, so it seems to me, carries the imprint of Torah.